TAILS OF joy

STORIES OF SPECIAL NEEDS ANIMALS
AND THE PEOPLE WHO ADOPTED THEM

GRETCHEN DALE

Photo Credits:
Front Cover: Maria Lovello
Author's photo: David Emberling
Sharon Honulik:pages 10,16,21,78,80,82,84,85,87,88,90,93,96
Paula Layton: page 9
David Rosenblum: page 99
Kathryn Schauer: page 34,41,60

ISBN: 0615987575
ISBN 13: 9780615987576

Library of Congress Control Number: 2014936079
Tails of Joy, Branford, CT

Special Thanks To

Susan Ariel Rainbow Kennedy who was my teacher and light on this journey. Thank you for all your wisdom and encouragement.

Goose and Tiny who told me I had to write this book.

Carl for never letting me give up on my journey.

All the adopters whose love, joy and friendship I will always cherish.

Special Note

The proceeds from this book will be donated to animal rescues and shelters so there will be more tails of joy in the world

Table *of* Contents

Introduction

Until one has loved an animal,
a part of one's soul remains unawakened.

—Anatole France

I was a busy corporate woman in a new job devoted to building a business in the United States for a large Chinese home textile company. I felt important and that I was one of the satisfied lucky ones with an exciting job. I soon found myself with a lot of mismatched towel samples that had collected in my home office. We were about to move to our new showroom and had no idea what to do with them. A friend suggested that I donate the towels to a local animal shelter, and so began an adventure that changed my life.

I soon became a volunteer at that shelter. This was the beginning of my journey of joy, love, and passion, and a complete devotion to something that had remained untouched in my soul until then. Over the next few years, a few hours of volunteering on a Saturday morning became four hours, then six hours, and finally spilled over into Sundays. I asked myself why. I did not get paid for my services. No one said, "Thank you." There was no visible benefit for me. Or was there?

Introduction

I came to realize that over my lifetime I had been judged by my accomplishments. First it was my grades and school achievements. Then it became my job promotions, salary, and even what I was wearing. As I moved up the corporate ladder, I took it for granted that I would be continually judged by others as well as by myself.

When I entered the world of animal rescue, I experienced for the first time what it was like not to be judged but to experience an animal's unconditional, nonjudgmental love. These animals did not care what I did, how much money I made, or how I was dressed. I believe that was what drew me further into this wonderful new place in my life, where my senses felt alive and my strength and determination abounded.

I did not realize at the time that one of the greatest joys I would ever know in my life would come from this new found passion. Every Saturday when I set foot in those kennels and looked into the faces of those abandoned animals, something beyond my control took possession of me. I had found what made me whole and real, and it had nothing to do with a big corporate job. It had to do with a pair of eyes that pierced my soul. At times I even felt addicted to the experience.

One could not ask for a better place to foster your spirits and feel joined with something more powerful than the human spirit. Animals are different from humans and their lives are set on a different course. They showed me a different way of looking at things. Thru them I found a different course in my own life that nourishes me beyond anything I have known.

Over the next years, I became more involved with rescue and adoption and found myself particularly drawn to animals with special needs. Some were behavioral needs, but most were medical. Animals don't know—or maybe don't care—when they are sick. They don't know why they misbehave because they have been locked in a crate for twelve hours a day while their owner is at work. What I soon found out was that shelters do not have the means or the time and staff to deal with these animals, and they are often euthanized. But I found myself unable to accept these shelter realities when brown eyes were piercing thru me as another unwanted life waned.

I set to work to do what I could to save some of these animals. While this was a personal journey, I was helped along the way by some very hard-working fellow volunteers, friends, and other rescuers—as well as by some very committed veterinarians who had the patience to help me. None of these stories would have been possible without all of their help.

I have also included stories that came to me from friends or contacts who wanted me to meet a special person who had rescued a special-needs animal. I would meet these people and their animals and know I had to include their stories, as well as my own personal stories. What a joy and an honor to have met all of these people and to be able to share their experiences.

In this book are some remarkable stories of these special-needs animals and the wonderful owners they found to take care of them. It is hard to believe that loving people were ever found to adopt these animals, yet all of them have told me over and over that they have received so much more from these animals than they have given. This book tells the stories not only of these special animals, but also of these special people who opened their hearts and awakened their souls.

This book is dedicated to all of the special-needs animals who have filled my life, but especially to *Goose -a* very small dog with a very big heart and gusto for life that knew no bounds.

I hope these stories please you and open your hearts and minds to a very special place that brings you joy and happiness, as they have for me. And I hope that these tales of joy will encourage you to adopt a special-needs animal and experience the love, joy, and happiness they can bring into your life. In today's world that is a very special wish I give to you..

Goose—
My Wonderful Boy

I was sitting at my desk at work one day and saw an e-mail pop up from another volunteer. Somehow I knew I was in trouble when the subject line read, "meet Goose, your kind of dog." I hit the jpeg to see the photo, and my heart just jumped. In front of me was a picture of a very senior, very tiny dog with a graying muzzle. He had such fire in his big, brown eyes. Those eyes seemed to see the whole world and to tell me his life's story in that photo. I closed the e-mail and prayed that he would be quickly adopted and I would not have to fall in love yet again. Sometimes this life with animals is exhausting, and I wanted a reprieve.

Fortunately, or unfortunately, the following Saturday I arrived at the shelter having not thought too much more of Goose. I wondered if he would be there. I hoped not. But I heard him before I saw him as I walked past the medical department. Then I knew why his name was Goose. If I had not known better, I would have thought we had taken in an injured goose when I heard the honking coming through the door. I slowly opened the door, and there in one of the kennels was a little guy who said to me, "I have seen the world, and in spite of what I have been through, I am a happy boy." I slowly opened the door, picked him up, and held him close. That was the end of my not thinking about him. In person, those eyes grabbed me right at the heart. I was his captive without question. Not another hour passed that he was not in my thoughts and in my heart.

I put Goose down on the floor, and he ran around making that silly honking sound. I laughed, but somehow I felt it was not funny. One of the staff came in and said, "Well, are you in love?"

"Yes," I said. "I am beyond in love."

I was completely wrapped up in Goose as his eyes drew me further and further in. The staff member then explained that he had been surrendered by animal control and that he had been found wandering the streets. They thought that, perhaps, he had been abandoned due to his age and heart condition. He had

no collar or tags. Abandoned! Is it truly possible any human would abandon a small animal like this in his condition? After all, he had given someone a lot of good years. I was somewhere between outraged and heartbroken.

I spent the better part of the morning with Goose, walking him in the sunshine and watching him take in his new world and surroundings like he was not afraid of anything. I learned, as I got to know him, that Goose was not afraid of much. He greeted each day with the gusto of a puppy, engaging everyone who came near him. He had a picky appetite, so we all started bringing in specially prepared chicken or beef, which he ate with great gusto. Soon we could not see his ribs anymore, and his coat started to look healthier.

Then I heard the words I never want to hear. He could not be put out for adoption as he had a very serious heart condition. In fact based on his age and condition, it was recommended he be put to sleep. My heart began racing, and I begged them not to do this and to give me some time to find someone who would adopt him. Realistically, I was saying to myself, "Where am I going to find anyone to adopt a very senior dog, with no teeth, who had congestive heart failure?" I cannot explain the emotions that overwhelmed me. I knew somehow I had to do this because Goose was counting on me.

I took Goose to the vet to get a confirmation of his condition. He held Goose and looked into his eyes. After confirming the serious heart condition, the vet said Goose could last a week or a month or a year. Then he said that Goose was one great little dog. That sealed it for me. Somehow I would tackle this job, and I would find a place for Goose to spend his last months with someone who would love him the way I did.

The next few days were a blur of networking. Did anyone know anyone who would take this wonderful dancing boy with the bark of a goose and care for him for whatever time he had left? It seemed like a stupid question, and I feared the answer would not be good. Most people, while sympathetic, were afraid to leave themselves vulnerable to falling in love with him only to lose him too quickly.

A few days later, a wonderful friend e-mailed me that she might know someone. A young lady who had another special-needs dog with a heart condition might be interested. I called my friend to confirm the news, as I could not believe my eyes reading her e-mail. She told me all about the young woman, Kim, and how she knew her. Still, I could not believe she would take a second dog with a heart condition. My friend described Kim as quiet, very in control, and very much what Goose would need. I broke my reserve and called Kim on the phone. She was exactly how my friend described her—calm, cool, asking all the right questions (including

expressing her concern about the cost of Goose's care). I told her Goose would require one pill a day and follow-up visits with the vet. Kim said she would probably do it, but would like to think a bit about it. I was happy to hear her recognize that this was a big step and a huge commitment. It showed me Kim was taking the potential adoption very seriously and wanted to make sure she was doing the right thing for herself and for Goose.

Several days later Kim called me to say she would like to adopt Goose. My heart soared! I was beyond joy! I was the happiest I had been in ages. Here was a young girl willing to help. We agreed I would take Goose to meet Kim on Saturday, as well as to meet her vet since we both knew he would be seeing a lot of Goose. The same volunteer who e-mailed me about Goose drove with me the two hours to Kim's house. Goose sat in my lap all the way, looking out the window, looking at me, and then napping. He seemed to know this was the next step in his life, and he was happy and peaceful with it.

When I met Kim that afternoon, I knew Goose was in the best of places. Kim appeared to be just what Goose needed. She was someone who had her act together enough to deal with him and to take care of him physically. I recognized her as someone who would love Goose until his dying day—which she did. I felt a pang as I turned to leave Goose and Kim. I loved Goose so much, and it was hard to say good-bye to him. But my heart was joyful that this wonderful little boy was joining Kim and her other dog, a Pomeranian named Tasha, to begin his new life. I knew Goose so well after all the time I had spent with him that I knew he would grasp every bit of life he could. He never realized how sick he really was.

Goose was now in a real home where he was able to enjoy life to its fullest, soaking in all of the love and joy Kim offered him. Tasha, Kim's other special-needs rescue, was not quite so thrilled to have another creature sharing Kim's love and affection. But like everyone who met Goose, it was hard for her not to fall in love with him. Tasha soon learned to accept Goose and allowed him to be part of the family. Kim knew that her time with Goose was short and valuable, and the threesome made the very most of it.

When Kim came home, Goose would greet her at the door barking that silly goose honk, dancing all around her in sheer exuberance as though he did not have a care in the world, and declaring to all that Kim was the center of his universe. Finally Kim would scoop him up in her arms and assure him that she was, in fact, his universe. Goose and Tasha were put on leashes for a walk, and it was a race out the door to see who could be the first to the sidewalk. Kim's neighbor would see this and say, "God bless him." You could not watch that little joyful body with the wagging, happy tail and look into his eyes that said, "I have been through so much" and not say that. He won over everyone who crossed his path with his total joy for life and love for every person that he met.

Goose was very small and at a stage in life when he had little but flesh and some thin fur covering his bones, yet he was as robust as any dog he came in contact with. When Kim had to take a business trip, she took Goose and Tasha to her sister's for a few days. When she called her sister to check on how they were all doing, her sister said Goose was bossing her big dogs around. Kim smiled and said, "That's my boy."

Several months later Kim said she could tell Goose was starting to slow down a little. Their walks were not the same. She would pick him up on the way back home because he was tired. Now Tasha was always the winner in the race to the sidewalk. Goose would muster up energy when he was back inside and it was time for his grilled chicken (which he loved almost as much as he loved life). Kim would get down on the floor and feed him. She reassured him he was her universe and she his. It was an incredible relationship.

But he continued to slow down. On Goose's final day with Kim, she said he followed her from room to room. He walked into the bedroom like he always would, looked around, and jumped into one of his many beds. He slept a little while she worked from home, not wanting to leave him. She had an uneasy feeling that something was happening.

Later on she wrapped him in a blanket, and he lay across her lap as she spoke to clients. Kim called the vet to prescribe something that she hoped would make him better. She left him only briefly to pick up the medication. When she returned she gave him the medicine and hand-fed him his favorite gourmet chicken. He ate very little.

"I knew our time was coming to an end, but my heart so wished I was wrong. He was such a huge part of my life," Kim shared with me. She laid him back on her lap, and he kept staring at her and nudging her with his nose as he often did when he wanted attention. She rubbed his head until he fell asleep. "Finally," Kim told me, "I placed his favorite igloo bed beside her bed and placed him in it."

Kim called me after that to tell me she did not think Goose would make it much longer. We both cried. I was sitting in my office sobbing. How could either of us let go of this tiny, helpless boy who had brought such joy and so many smiles to our hearts?

At midnight Tasha barked. Kim turned on the light, and her wonderful, dearest Goose was gone. She told me the next day how sad she had been but how peaceful and happy Goose looked, even in leaving her.

"Goose was my loyal and wonderful friend," said Kim. "I wish I could have had him longer, but I am so very grateful for the time I had with him. He taught me so much about life and grabbing all the joy it has to offer. He made me realize that, even when the world does not always touch us gently, there are still gentle things in the world that touch us deeply."

The next morning when I received the email from Kim telling me about Goose's peaceful and loving passing, I cried again. I took the picture that was in that email and put it in my purse where it remains to this day. His picture keeps the hole he left from feeling so empty.

Kim is a very special person to have accepted Goose into her life along with all that came with him. She was grounded beyond belief and compassionate beyond words. Kim and Goose were a perfect pair, and I knew it from the first moment I saw them together. Kim told me many times she never regretted for one moment taking Goose. She said he returned her love and compassion a hundred fold. He was her philosopher, teacher, comedian, and love all rolled into a tiny, little body. But inside that body was the biggest heart one could imagine—a heart that found joy in everything.

Kim and I have stayed in contact since Goose died. We laugh about the silly, wonderful things he did, and we laugh about his funny honking bark. We talk about the joy he brought to each of us and how he taught us about life—how to grasp it and enjoy it to the fullest. I am so very thankful that I met Kim because of Goose. It makes me smile to think he left us the joy of friendship. What more could we ask of that tiny boy with that great big heart?

Goose inspired me to write this book, and that was his special gift to me. He touched my soul and has made me want to tell others how much adopting a special-needs animals can change their lives. Special-needs animals take us out of ourselves and put us in a different place where the world is gentle and caring and where the sun shines even on a rainy day. Loving these animals is loving yourself. Respecting these animals is respecting yourself.

Tango the Pedengo with Megaesophagus! (Say That Three Times Fast)

As I set off to the shelter one Saturday morning, I was anxious to see the new group of dogs that had been brought in from one of our local animal control shelters. It is always quite interesting to see the mix of cute and not-so-cute, the crazy mixes-big and small-and often a pit bull or two to challenge me. So I was smiling as I was driving saying, "I wonder what I will find in those kennels today? Bring them on, pit bulls and all."

As I came down the hallway, I looked through a window and saw a very skinny, white and tan, scruffy-looking dog. His huge brown eyes were totally out of proportion to his skinny body, each rib clearly visible. My first thought was that he must have been starved to look like this. How could anyone starve a dog, especially one as cute as this? As I entered to take him for a walk, I saw his name was Tango. He stood up and wagged his tail, which made his whole body wiggle. He had very long legs, cute, curly, terrier-type hair, and, oh, those brown eyes. I was captured the minute I looked into them.

The eyes of an animal tell so much. They hold his whole life in a look. They told me he was scared and had seen a lot in his few short years, but they also told me he was loving and sweet, and just wanted to be touched and loved. Those eyes seemed to be begging for love and care. And then I noticed he had thrown up his last meal, but I did not think too much about it. It often happens with our new recruits.

We set off for our morning walk. Tango was happy and playful. I came upon one of our caring staff members, who said there was something wrong with Tango. He could not keep any food down. Maria, another volunteer, came over and was also interested in what the staff member was saying, as she too had fallen for this scruffy-looking, brown-eyed boy when she met him a few days earlier. Maria and I sat with Tango for a while and marveled at how silly looking he was and I think at that moment we both made an unspoken pact that we would do whatever had to be done to get him well and to find him a good home. Little did we know how challenging that was going to be.

When we went back inside, we put Tango in the small bathing room and fixed a comfortable bed for him hoping he could rest without all the noise and confusion of the kennel environment. Over the next few days, the vet examined him, but there were no specific signs of anything wrong with him. Yet every time he would eat, he would very soon begin to salivate and throw up. By the way, it did not stop him from eating, and he continued to be happy and playful throughout this ritual.

The verdict came back from the veterinarian that he could not find the cause of Tango's vomiting and there was really nothing more that could be done. Hearing those words, our hearts sank. Maria and I looked at each other and, without a word, we kicked into gear with a complete resolve to take charge of this wonderfully sweet boy and do whatever it took to get to the bottom of the situation. Our love for this young dog would not let us give up on him, and love makes difficult tasks possible. We formulated our plans and asked our district manager if we could put our plan in motion. She, too, had fallen victim to his charm, and she was pretty easy to convince.

Here was the plan: Maria would foster Tango, and we would see if being out of the shelter environment might help. We would also take him to my vet and get another medical opinion. Sounded like an easy plan. But at 3:00 a.m. one morning, I got an e-mail from Maria saying Tango had thrown up everywhere. The next morning I called my vet, and Maria brought Tango over for an exam. Surely he would be able to fix whatever was wrong with Tango. After a thorough exam, the vet said he thought the problem might be one of two things. Based on his almost-hoarse bark, he thought Tango had perhaps been chained up for a long period, pulled on the chain, and damaged his throat. His second thought was that he might have ingested a toxic substance such as antifreeze. We discussed our options and decided further tests might be needed to determine the cause of the problem. If it were one of these two causes, though, there would not be much could do to make him better.

The following day another one of our volunteers e-mailed us and said she had done some research on the Internet. Tango's symptoms seemed to be those of megaesophagus. I had never heard of this condition, could not pronounce it, and definitely could not spell it. But my heart sank to think Tango had something that seemed very serious when I read about the disease on the website she forwarded to me. How could a dog that seemed to be so happy have a disease I could not even pronounce?

I then went online and learned that megaesophagus is a very rare disease that has several causes. Some of the causes might be able to be treated, but often the only treatment is for the dog to eat pureed food. The muscle of the esophagus is weakened and does not push the food down to the stomach. Instead, the food stays in the esophagus. Maria kicked right into gear and talked to several people who gave us some good advice about a high calorie food mix that could be pureed. If we could get his meals to stay down, he might put on some weight. Just as we thought we had the answer, we read further and learned that megaesophagus dogs need to eat in a standing position and stay that way for twenty minutes after they eat. Staying in an upright position allows all the food to go down to the stomach instead of lodging in the esophagus. My heart raced to think that perhaps we had found a solution. How were we ever going to make it work, though?

Maria and I talked at length and, again, called the vet and told him what we had found. He said he was familiar with megaesophagus, but had never examined a dog that had it. We visited the vet again, and so began a very long process of tests to determine if Tango's condition was truly megaespophagus and, if so, what kind.

Maria began feeding Tango by placing his food bowl on the top rung of a stepstool. He ate standing and patiently listened to Maria as she encouraged him to stay in that position for twenty minutes after eating. Maria diligently held him upright each time he ate.

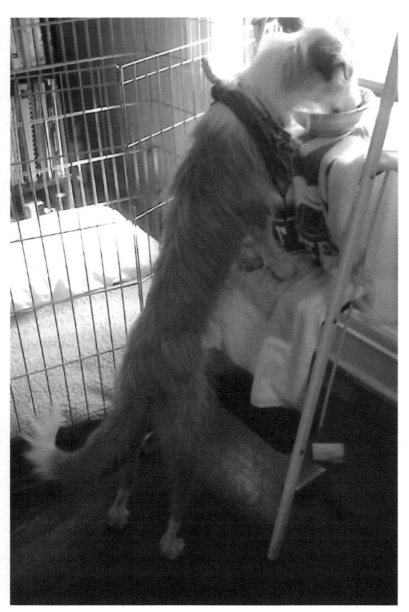

Slowly Tango began to hold down more of his food, and—before our eyes—he began to put on some weight. One night I got one of my regular e-mails from Maria, but this one said that Tango did not throw up at all that night. Could it really be? Somewhere in the middle of this celebration, Maria put a blue bandanna around Tango's neck. It was his badge of courage, and it soon became his signature. From that point on, he was never without a bandanna. It was as if it said, "I am going to conquer all you put in front of me, and I am going to love you for helping me do this." Maria sent me photos of him wearing that bandanna and looking so much better. My heart swelled to think how far he had come and how truly wonderful it was to see the transformation. For one, short moment my mind said he was not sick and would be well in no time.

Tango endured several tests to see if this was really this dreaded disease, and reality set in quickly for us when we confirmed via an endoscopy that he did, in fact, have the pockets in his esophagus, and he did have the disease we could not pronounce! While we suffered under the news, Tango continued to be his energetic, playful, and happy self. Those of us who loved him so were devastated, but Tango did not let it bother him. He soon thought every dog stood up to eat and stood up on a step stool till their Mom said he could get down. And his adapting to all of this taught us a great deal about his spirit and it set in us a spirit that we would not give up on him for any reason at all.

Maria and I wondered, who in this world would ever adopt a dog with a disease like this that required a specially blended and prepared diet and a daily routine of feeding him standing up? Looking at this crazy, wonderful boy wearing the bandanna on his neck and romping in Maria's yard, we knew somehow, someway, we had to find him his forever home.

A forever home! It seemed like a pretty unachievable task. Maria continued to foster Tango as his picture and story went up on the shelter website and on Petfinder. We made a giant poster for the front of the shelter, as

well, to entice potential adopters to at least ask about Tango. Several people did inquire, and he even had an interaction with a family. While they found him charming, they had some severe doubts and decided he was not for them. Maria's husband, Frank, had just about decided that they might in fact become Tango's forever home when Sara and Brook contacted the shelter through the Petfinder site. Was it possible this would be a great fit? We tried not to get our hopes up.

Brook and Sara had a perfect Boston terrier named Barnaby and had been looking for a second dog. They had previously considered a special needs, hard-to-adopt dog. They found an ad for two Chihuahuas that had no front legs and responded, but they never heard back from the rescue. One day someone from their neighborhood called and said they had found Barnaby. Brook and Sara were both away from the house and were puzzled how Barnaby could have gotten out, but they rushed over only to find a perfect Barnaby look-alike. They took him home and started thinking about what to name this sweet, well-behaved boy. They would keep him if they could not find his owner. But four days later the family turned up and was beyond happy to have their pet back. And so Brook and Sara went back to their search for that special dog.

Brook found Tango on Petfinder and read his story to Sara who said, "Don't show me, please, it is too sad." So what did Brook do? She enlarged Tango's photo and put it in front of Sara. Sara said she melted when she saw that funny-looking, brown-eyed boy wearing the blue bandanna.

They called and made an appointment to see Tango the very next day, and on Saturday morning they ventured out to meet Tango and Maria at the shelter. They followed Maria and Frank back to their house to see the feeding ritual they would have to adopt for Tango. Barnaby came along as well. When he ran into the house to greet everyone, Tango came over and bit him. Not a very good start for a dog looking for his forever home. Maria explained Tango's situation, including the elaborate food preparation and feeding process. Sara said she was totally stressed out and intimidated, but something about Tango drew her in. They decided to go home and think about it.

As they turned to leave, Frank said, "You don't have to take him. Nothing will happen to him if you don't." He must have sensed their hesitancy and wanted them to know Tango was special, and he would be safe till the right home was found.

As Brook and Sara drove home, they deliberated about whether Tango's care was too much to take on; however, by the next morning they both realized that Tango was theirs—for better or for worse—and they headed back to Maria's to take him home. They left Maria's house with Tango, all his food and instructions, his wire pen for nighttime, and his favorite stuffed rabbit.

The next weeks were tough as Tango tried to fit into their lives and they tried to cope with Tango's special needs. It wasn't easy. Tango threw up often, and soon he had hit just about every rug in the house. Brook said the vomit was the consistency and look of a jellyfish and very hard to clean up with paper towels. They soon learned to use a dustpan and brush, which was far more effective. Ever so slowly things began to calm down a bit. Barnaby also struggled thru a period of adjustment of not being the only dog in the house. It took some time but Barnaby and Tango made peace and became good friends who enjoyed running together in the park and just chilling out at home. Tango's throwing up became less and was no longer a multiple times a day occurance. Tango did choose to have one of his worst episodes—right on top of their newly made bed—just before they left for their wedding ceremony. Off came the bedding and the couple cleaned up another "jelly fish," as it came to be called.

At first Sara and Brook followed Maria's dog food recipes. As time went on, they found they could give Tango ground beef and baked sweet potato that was not pureed. Soon he was eating treats and keeping them down. One thing that did not change was Tango's need to stand up on the stepstool to eat. It was Tango's ritual, and he did it without too much coaching. As he saw his food being prepared, he would tap dance around the kitchen, climb up the stepstool with his front paws, and begin to drool as he stood waiting for his food. Sara and Brook's apartment overlooked the bus stop near Yale in New Haven, and Tango's stepstool was at the window overlooking a lot of activity. Tango would eat his meal then put his head down on the top rung and watch all the activity going on outside. He became a regular at the window, wearing his scarf and staring out at everyone. Little did he or anyone outside know that he was not a normal, average dog. Passersby saw only a cute, scruffy dog with big, brown eyes and a bandanna. His signature bandanna has become his trademark. He doesn't always wear a blue bandanna now, but he always wears one.

Things began to settle down. A few days would pass and Tango would not have thrown up. But just as things started to seem normal, he began to have some seizures—a couple the first year, and then they became more frequent. The seizures would last about ten minutes, and Tango would flail around. Brook said it was quite scary at times. But when the seizure was over, Tango seemed his normal self. Sara and Brook learned to hydrate Tango with ringer's solution, which helped a bit, but Tango was soon diagnosed with idiopathic epilepsy and the seizures became more frequent. Their vet put him on phenobarbital and the seizures have subsided, at least for now.

Tango has made great progress in spite of everything. He has gained weight. He is happy and now actually comes and greets people rather than shying away. And, surprisingly, we learned that Tango was not a scruffy little mutt at all, but was actually a breed called a Podengo, which originated in Portugal.

One day Brook and Sara came across the most incredible thing while playing in the local park with Tango and Barnaby they came across a woman whose friend had two dogs that looked just like Tango. She introduced Brook and Sara to her friend and soon they met both dogs. Romeo who looked just like Tango and his sister, Juliette, also looked a lot like Tango. More incredible was the fact that Romeo had megaesophagus just like Tango and Juliette had seizures just like Tango. Now the owners of all the dogs have found a support group. Like Tango, Romeo does not seem to think there is anything at all wrong with him and neither does Juliette. It is pretty neat to see all three of these Podengos together—a breed most people have never seen. A final, amazing fact is that both Romeo and Juliette were rescue dogs just like Tango. Brook and Sara marvel and wonder if, perhaps, the dogs are related.

Tango would have been way too much work for most people, but Brook and Sara have worked through a lot to give this wonderful boy as normal a life as possible. They love him with all their hearts. I asked them if they ever had any doubts about taking on Tango. Brook admits from time to time she has had a few. I asked if they would ever give him up and got a unified response, "Oh, God, no!"

Brook said, as a child, she felt like a ragamuffin kid. She sees in Tango so much of what she was as a child. Sara spent a lot of time around special needs humans and she said, "I don't see Tango as that different. He is a bit of an outcast and a mess, but I don't judge him that way. He needs someone who won't judge him. I feel a total responsibility to Tango." As she says this, tears well in my eyes that she and Brook could feel this way about a dog that is such a challenge, but such an incredible companion.

I went back to Brook and Sara's apartment one night after we had met to talk about Tango. I wanted to see him and see if he was as I remembered. As we entered there he was with those big, brown eyes the soft, light-brown nose, and that stuffed-animal, scruffy coat. He came up to me and, as he had done the very first time I met him, he warmed my heart as I stared into those beautiful eyes and saw the special soul that lives behind them. Nothing had changed about how he affected all those he came in contact with.

Tango is still afraid of wood floors and backs up onto rugs to avoid them whenever possible. Brook and Sara say he really does not have very good life skills. He ate a stick of butter the other day, wrapper and all. He chases trucks; he walks without bending his legs, but—altogether—he makes one very special dog. Tango has fought against all odds. He has found an incredible life and makes everyone who comes in contact with him smile and laugh. That is a pretty special thing for a dog whose life was hanging in the balance a few years before. Like so many of these special needs animals, he has taught me that they do not dwell on their infirmity, but rather they share joy and love with all those they come in contact with.

As I was leaving, Sara took off Tango's bandanna and told me to wait a moment. Several minutes later she brought the scarf back out, and Tango danced with excitement and came over to have her put it on his neck. It is his badge of courage. I smiled from ear-to-ear as I kissed him good-bye and left to go home. I knew this special dog had a special reason for being who he is and where he is—raising joy for all those he comes in contact with. Tango the Padengo, thank you for letting me be part of your life. And thank you Brook and Sara for not judging Tango as different, but instead for loving him to the fullest exactly like he is.

Tiny—
Little Curmudgeon

Usually it is the eyes that grab me first in a rescue animal, but for Tiny it was not that at all. His eyes were bloodshot and very clouded over. There were huge, black-looking circles in the fur around them. He was a little Shih Tzu with the most curious stride I had ever seen, and his legs looked crooked and bent like a little old man. What hit me first, though, was his smell. He smelled like very old cheese! It made my nose wrinkle up and my eyes squeeze shut.

The odor was not pleasant, to say the least. But something about Tiny wrapped around my heart and my better judgment, and I picked him up. He stuck his head in the crook of my neck and from that moment we became one and the same spirit. Tiny was my boy! And he let everyone know it. I loved him no matter how he smelled—and that is saying a lot about what love can overcome. Whenever he saw me, he would come running with his strange swagger and crooked legs. He would sit on my feet and squeal to be picked up and loved. My heart would leap for joy every time he did this.

My relationship with Tiny became an ongoing saga that would keep the two of us together for a very long time in search of something to cure his skin condition. Our vet tested Tiny to see if he could find the cause of the problem. We kept his fur shaved short, but his skin was very greasy, and he had little, black peppery specks all over him. From time to time, he would develop pustules on his skin that would break and bleed. One day when I came to walk him, he came out holding his front, right paw off the ground. He was the most pathetic-looking, little curmudgeon I had ever seen, but he came running toward me anyway on his three legs. This pathetic sight wrenched my whole being. As I bent down to look at his paw, I saw a pustule between his toes. His enthusiastic greeting melted my heart, and I vowed then that we would find out what was happening to him.

I took my little, rag-tag boy to my vet to see what he would say. He didn't have to say much. His facial expression said it all when he got a whiff of Tiny. He thought the odor might possibly be caused by a thyroid issue. In the following days, I started giving Tiny medication and using special shampoos, but he was only marginally better. Tiny and I then visited many other vets in search of someone who could help him. One of our staff members thought Tiny might have a compromised immune system that was causing his problems, so we started investigating that possibility. Over time Tiny became part of our shelter family, and all the staff seemed to become his advocates. I finally came to the realization that if no one would adopt my Tiny boy, then he would come live with me. But I also knew that Tiny had so much to offer someone if we could just get rid of his odor.

Tiny loved being outside in the sun, and it seemed to help his skin a bit. So the Staff created a special little pen for him where he could be outside much of the day. Because of his poor eyesight, he tended to become anxious when he was inside and not around humans, but outside he seemed to find his special place where he began to relax and enjoy life. While his skin improved a bit from all the special baths and his time in the fresh air and sun, we really were no further along in the journey to a solution than we had been several months before.

Then one day a older gentleman came in and adopted him. We explained Tiny's difficulties, but Tiny and this man had that special chemistry when they met. He believed he could deal with the challenges that came along with his new friend. And so Tiny went home with this man. They were a great pair of curmudgeons but, unfortunately, his family was not able to overlook Tiny's condition and the resulting odor. There were no answers we could give to Tiny's new owner. He loved Tiny, but he could not handle this special-needs boy, so back Tiny came to the shelter. While everyone was very sad that Tiny did not find his forever home, everyone welcomed him back like an old veteran. He was safe and cared for here and loved in spite of his condition.

I realized, however, love was not enough for Tiny! We had to do more. I took Tiny home to foster for a few weeks to see if being out of the shelter environment might help him. We worked on a special diet and some antianxiety herbal medicines, and they all helped—but only marginally. I loved him every day, but due to the unknown cause of his condition I did not want to let him near my senior dog, and Tiny was not

happy being separated from the rest of my family. He would cry and whine when I left him alone, and that broke my heart. We gave him the nickname Tiny Whiny, which stuck with him for a very long time. After several weeks of no real improvement, I brought him back to the shelter to see if we could solve this ongoing mystery.

Enter Ponus a senior, blind beagle. All of us gravitated to him and wondered how we would ever get him adopted. Senior dogs hold a very special place in our hearts. So several days after his arrival, Ponus met Tiny and we allowed them in the outdoor pen together. From then on Tiny and Ponus spent many contented hours in the special pen enjoying all that the outdoors had to offer. Tiny even with his poor eyesight was Ponus's eyes and Ponus was Tiny's comfort. Together they were two kindred curmudgeons against the world.

I was glad Tiny had a new canine buddy, but I was still intent on finding the root of his skin condition. In sheer frustration, I took Tiny back to my vet. He said he did not know what was wrong with Tiny, and there was only one vet he knew who might be able to unlock our mystery. This new lead was a ray of hope but, as Tiny and I rode back to the shelter together, I tried not to get my hopes up. He sat in the front seat looking at me like he was taking in every word I was saying. When I got back to the shelter, I told everyone the latest. I saw my own discouragement reflected in the faces around me when I reported the lack of progress from the most recent vet's visit. I then explained that we had one more road open to us, and I shared our next step.

The next day I called the phone number of my "last hope" vet and found it would be two weeks before I could get Tiny an appointment. I waited, hoping against hope that this time we would finally find an answer to Tiny' medical problem. Once again, Tiny got into the front seat of my car and gave me a "let's get it over with" look. Kim (a staff member who had fallen under Tiny's spell just as I did) came with us. I looked over at Kim, and she had the same look of concern on her face that I felt. Our hearts were jumping with hope, but our heads were wondering if this was another dead end. And, if so, where would we turn next.

We were escorted into the examining room, and my "last chance" vet took one look and got one whiff and exclaimed, "Oh wow!" My heart sank. She started examining Tiny with a fine-tooth comb and asked if anyone had given him a deep skin scraping. I did not recall any other vet doing that so she asked her assistant to come in and they held Tiny tightly and scraped his skin. The vet went to her lab room, and we waited for the results of our last hope. If we didn't solve the puzzle this time, I was at the end of my options. I was so worried about this funny, little boy who sat in my lap looking up at me wondering what in the world had just happened to him. My little curmudgeon just wanted to get in the car and go home. And so did I.

Then the vet came around the corner and asked Kim and me to come take a look in the microscope. "Do you see those little things swimming around?" she asked. "Those are mites." At that point I felt relieved we had a diagnosis, but I did not know exactly what it meant. She explained at length that all dogs have mites, but they usually don't create problems since a healthy dog's immune system keeps them in check. She said that Tiny's compromised immune system was not strong enough to do that. She indicated that he would need to be treated with some pretty serious meds and that he would probably be on them for rest of his life. These drugs were fairly expensive, so now we had another adoption hurdle to overcome. In addition, the vet prescribed six weeks of antibiotics to control the cysts while the potent medicine began to control the mites. She said we would also need to bathe Tiny weekly in a special shampoo—and this, too, would be a lifelong requirement.

In spite of the sobering protocol, we headed back to the shelter with something we hadn't had in nearly a year—*hope*. When we arrived back at the shelter, Tiny looked at us like we were all crazy as we laughed and hugged this little boy. I took him outside, and he was far more excited about seeing his buddy, Ponus, than about what had just happened. It was then I realized that neither Ponus nor Tiny cared that Tiny smelled and that Ponus was blind. They were each other's greatest comfort. As I watched them sitting in the sun with each other, I had a feeling that things were going to change for both of them.

Tiny started on his new meds and his weekly baths and his continued eye drops. Fortunately, Tiny loves to be loved and touched, so administering all of his special care was not difficult. And after a few weeks he started to look and feel much better.

I was out of town and got a call from the district manager that Tiny's previous owner had called. He asked if Tiny was still with us and, if so, if we would consider allowing him to readopt Tiny. He was back on his feet and more than anything wanted to have Tiny back in his life. This was not a common thing for the shelter to do but Tiny had been thru so much and so had his owner that it was agreed Tiny could go back home

with him. Our shelter told Tiny's owner about all the medications and other special care that Tiny would now need. He understood and said he would be able to handle it. The following Saturday morning, his owner came to pick him up. Tiny was outside with Ponus and, while my heart was so happy for Tiny, my heart sank when I looked at Ponus and realized he was going to lose his best friend in the whole world. It was a bittersweet moment; I was jumping for joy for Tiny, and crying inside my heart for Ponus.

Off Tiny went to try and pick up the pieces of his life. I went back outside to see Ponus after Tiny left, and I could tell he knew that his best friend was not coming back. I sat with him and tried to explain. He looked up at me, as though he could see, and said with those blind eyes, "It is OK. I will miss him, but I am so happy for my friend." Several days later a wonderful family who did not care that Ponus was blind adopted him. Who needs eyes when you have such a big heart? So both the curmudgeon boys were gone from the shelter. We all missed them, but we all knew it was a good kind of missing.

Several years later I got a message from Kim saying, "Guess who is back?" I knew immediately that it had to be Tiny, but all I could think of was that it just couldn't be. Tiny's owner was moving overseas and could not take Tiny with him. Tiny was there when I arrived for my Saturday volunteer day, but this time he looked and smelled like a different dog. He ran over with his curmudgeon strut and crooked legs and we picked up right where we left off. The following weekend he and I packed into the car to visit the "last hope" vet so she could see his progress and determine whether or not he could be off the meds now.

When she saw Tiny, she absolutely did not recognize him by looks or smell. She was amazed at his progress, but she was not hopeful he could be off the skin medication. So back we went to the shelter, and up he went for adoption, again, as a special-needs dog. He looked great, but who was going to want to have him along with all his baggage?

Tiny must be a really special curmudgeon, because I got a text message that a woman named Susan had seen him on the website and was coming to visit. She was looking for a friend for her dog, Baby, an eight-year-old bichon frise. I did not get my hopes up (and maybe deep down I hoped no one would adopt him and I would have to). Who would want a dog with poor eyesight and a continuing skin problem anyway?

Susan came to the shelter and, with no idea of adopting a special-needs dog, she fell for him just like we all had. She spent several hours there and really did not want to leave without him. As Susan sat on the floor holding and playing with Tiny, it was apparent to all that the two had already bonded. Susan had four cats at home (several of whom were rescued) but Tiny was ambivalent to cats, so that was not a problem. Baby didn't seem to give Tiny much trouble during their interaction, so off Tiny went to try again to see if he could become part of a real family.

I had not been at the shelter the day Susan adopted Tiny, and before she left the staff told Susan about me and asked if it would be all right if I got in touch with her to see how they were both doing. Susan said that she would like to meet Tiny's other mom. So one day we met for lunch and shared our stories about this wonderful, little man.

Susan's three children are all grown and out of the house. Rather than enjoying an empty nest Susan and her husband, Dean, decided to provide foster care for a brother and sister who needed a second chance. Susan said she came from a difficult background herself and that helping these kids—and now Tiny—just seemed like it was right thing to do. Dean and Susan have a lot of love to share, and they are very generous with it. They now have an extended family with lots of people, noise, and animals going in and out all day. It is a perfect place for a Tiny little curmudgeon.

Susan said she feels like Tiny is, in a way, like her and her foster kids. They all came out of a bad situation and have turned things around when someone gave them the chance. My heart eased, and I knew from that comment alone that Tiny had found his forever home with just the right family. Susan named Tiny "Benji" as she felt he needed a new name for his new life with their family. And I loved the fact that Susan referred to me as Benji's other mom. I was thrilled that this very special animal was now part of a family that would love him more than I could ever have hoped.

Susan told me Benji has two nicknames now: Broken and Joker. He earned the nickname "Broken" because he does not do what most dogs do. He doesn't bark, he doesn't eat treats, he doesn't play with toys or do other things most dogs do, so her kids say he is a broken dog. I loved the name; it fit him perfectly. These things never seemed to be part of his life. What he most enjoys is to sit next to those he loves and take a nap. And maybe that makes him only a little broken! He is sometimes referred to lovingly as "Joker" because when he is enjoying himself, he has a smile from ear-to-ear just like the Joker from Batman. I smiled when I heard both of these nicknames, because they so describe this little guy. Susan has one more special nickname that she alone uses: "My Little Man."

Like so many of the special-needs rescuers I have met, Susan said, "I truly feel blessed to be rescued by Benji. He has issues, but they are very small compared to what they could be. He is no different than you and I. We all have had, or will have, problems in our lifetime, and animals are no different. If I can make Benji healthier and comfortable, it is a small price for what he has given me and my family."

Susan said all of this to me at lunch that day, and her eyes were bright and full of love for her family and for this very special little boy. She then related a story about a day recently when the family out kayaking. Benji was along for the ride and, since it was a very hot day, she put Benji into the lake to cool off and to see if he could swim. At first he started to sink, but he soon realized if he started paddling he could swim. He loved it, and she said that when he reached the area where he could stand up, he turned to her with his big Joker smile on his face.

As I drove home from my lunch with Susan, I thought about all we had talked about. My heart wanted to burst with joy knowing that, finally, this little man had found a true place for himself with a family. They accept all his funny

and quirky traits and still want to love him and care for him. A tear rolled down my check—a tear of thanks and joy for people like Susan who step forward to salvage the lives of these animals.

Thank you Susan, Dean, and family for loving this funny, little curmudgeon as much as his shelter family loved him. Thank you for seeing him for so much more than a special-needs animal. And thank you, Benji, for bringing Susan and me together. Our love for you is a bond we will always share.

Shorey—
A Dog with a "Just Do It" Attitude

Over the many years I have been involved in rescue, there have been some animals that I simply couldn't resist trying to help. Shorey was one of these special ones. I found it incredible that, in spite of severe injury, he could look straight at me with a calm, stoic demeanor that pulled me right into his world. Maybe that is because Shorey was a lot like me. In the worst of times, I sometimes seem to pull strength from within and just do what needs to be done. Since my childhood I had drawn great strength from helping sick and injured animals. My mother used to sigh when I would come to the door with yet another fallen bird or an injured squirrel, but she could not talk me out of helping them.

Shorey's story is truly remarkable. He had been hit by a car on Shore road, hence his name. He lay under a bush for several days until a local resident stopped after realizing what she had thought was a black plastic bag was not. When she pulled over, she found a severely injured dog. She called our local animal control officer (ACO), and an officer named Laura came out immediately and transported Shorey to the emergency vet clinic. The veterinarian found that Shorey's spinal cord was severely injured. Back surgery was needed as soon as possible since the accident had happened several days earlier.

Laura is an incredible ACO officer and animal advocate, but her city budget did not have the funds to provide the extensive medical care that Shorey needed. Laura never gives up on an animal in need, so she sent a mass e-mail asking for donations. Time was of the essence so, instead of waiting for donations to come in, the decision was made to proceed with the surgery. We decided we would raise the funds needed to cover the surgery somehow—even if we had to bake a million brownies or stand on a street corner asking for donations. Like Shorey, we put on our "just do it" attitude, and there was no doubt in any of our minds or hearts that we could raise the funds.

Several weeks later Shorey left the veterinary clinic and went to our local animal shelter, and I decided I had to go see him. Laura told me he had been doing great, but I needed to see for myself. When I entered the shelter, I saw Shorey behind the front desk lying on his bed. There was no moping alone in his kennel to recuperate for him. He made himself right at home in the middle of all the people coming and going through the shelter. Shorey looked up at me with his big eyes and slowly came over to me with his head bowed. He had a very long shaved row down his back with an equally long row of staples. He raised his head and gave me a look that said, "Don't worry about me. I had to get all these staples in my back so I can get better, and I am going to be OK." But my heart went out to him as he stood so bravely in front of me. I could not believe his steadfast calm and his "just do it" attitude.

No one ever came to claim Shorey, which was hard for me to believe. His story had been in the paper and on TV, but still no one came. We all loved him, but he was truly alone after all he had been through and that saddened me. No animal should ever suffer that fate, especially with all the inner strength he had demonstrated. As he got better came the task of finding Shorey a home where he would be loved and no longer alone. Finding someone who would consider taking a dog with a back injury was not going to be an easy task. But somewhere there had to be someone who would find a place for this big-eyed wonder boy.

A few weeks later, we held a fundraiser at my home to finish raising the last of the funds for Shorey's back surgery. I asked Laura if she would bring Shorey to the fundraiser, and she agreed. I felt we could really tell his story better and raise more money if those that attended could actually meet him. There he was in the middle of twenty-five ladies and with typical calmness, he went to each visitor, unprompted, and introduced himself. He accepted pats on the head, and he listened to each the woman as if he understood every word. He was a true ambassador for rescue dogs everywhere that evening as he sought out a lap to rest his head or a hand to lick.

As Laura told the group about Shorey and what he had been through, they were introduced to the good work that our local animal shelter does for the animals they take in. Laura explained that it is only through the generosity of our local citizens that these special needs animals can be saved. As Shorey continued mingling, there was a sense of sadness for what he had been through. But as he went from person-to-person, that sad cloud became a smile on the face of each person he met. When Shorey finished making his rounds, Laura announced that he had found his forever home and would be going to his new family in a few days. My heart jumped at this news, and all I could think about was the possibility of getting to meet Shorey's new family. Several months later, I had the opportunity to meet these special people.

Deb and her husband, Eric, had been looking quite some time for another dog to bring into their lives. Deb had lost her most wonderful friend Rudy, a seventeen-year-old shepherd-mix rescue dog, several years earlier. But she was finding it hard to find a dog that could fill the hole he had left in her heart. Rudy had been Deb's dog, but when Eric and his daughter came into Deb's life, Rudy rapidly became part of the whole family. His death had left them all hurting, but their current lifestyle was hectic, and Eric's daughter was heading off to college. They all agreed this was not a time for a new dog in their lives. Instead Deb began to volunteer at the shelter on weekends, where she put her love of dogs to good work. Eric told me that, after Deb had been volunteering for a while, she sat him down and made it very clear that she wanted another dog in her life. They began to foster dogs, and Deb introduced Eric to some of the dogs she met at the shelter, but nothing really clicked.

It was not until two and a half years later when Deb came in for her regular Saturday morning volunteer shift at the shelter that Laura said, "Deb, I think I have your dog." Out came Shorey, staples and scars and all. Deb felt something she had not felt since she had lost her beloved Rudy, and she went home to tell Eric.

Deb soon took Eric to the shelter to meet this incredible survivor with the big, brown eyes. Eric confessed to me it was not love at first sight, but he too had experienced back surgery several years earlier, and he felt a tug toward this amazing dog who was recovering so well. He put his hand on Shorey's back and said to Deb, "This is the first dog I would think about adopting." After several more visits Deb and Eric agreed that Shorey was to be part of their family. They filled out the adoption papers and off they went to start their life together.

The first few weeks with Shorey were a bit tentative. Shorey stayed mostly in his bed and was low profile. As always he was very composed and self-contained. Eric described him as being a bit on the serious side. But little-by-little Shorey began to come to life in his new surroundings with his new family. Eric's daughter came home from college and liked Shorey very much. She convinced her parents that they needed to change Shorey's name to reflect his new life instead of to remind him of his past life. And so the family chose "Hunter," after Hunter S. Thompson the writer.

Hunter loved walks with Eric and Deb, and he loved every dog and person he came in contact with as they walked. Woods surrounded his new home, and Hunter was eager to run and experience all the sights and smells they had to offer. But Eric and Deb had been told he could not be off leash and play freely because of his back. They were very concerned, and did not know how they would handle his not being able to play with other dogs—let alone chase all the creatures that inhabited the woods. So Eric, Deb, and Hunter set off to see the vet who had performed the back surgery. The news was good. Hunter was completely healed, and it would be fine to let him off his leash to run and play. Eric and Deb were ecstatic that they could let Hunter begin to enjoy life again without being held back.

Eric took Hunter into the woods the next day and took off his leash. Eric felt a moment of trepidation, but from the moment the leash was released, Eric says Hunter's true personality came out. Amazingly, he obeyed all of Eric's commands. He loved to run and play and chase some of the animals—especially the deer—but he would always come back when he heard Eric call. He always returned with a big smile on his face, as if he was possessed with happiness. During these adventures Eric realized that Hunter and he had become the very best of friends.

Soon Hunter discovered the wonders of the squirrel-buster bird feeder, and he would sit and bark all night at the raccoons that came to steal the birdseed. In order to keep the peace, Eric started taking the feeder into the house every night. It was a bit of craziness, but a whole lot better than hearing Hunter bark at the raccoons all night long. During the day, Hunter loves to sit on the deck, put his head through the railing, and bite the branches of the bushes on the other side and pull them through the railing to the deck. Eric says this is a side of Hunter that no one really knew existed. He is comical and loves to do funny, harmless things that have no rationale. This funny side of Hunter makes him all the more endearing, as it is the opposite of his calm, stoic side.

Eric and Deb spend a lot of time in New York City, due to their careers. They originally planned to get a dog sitter when they were away, but it soon became apparent that this was not a fair thing to do to Hunter after all he had been through. Eric reworked his schedule so he could take Hunter into New York City with him to see how Hunter would do as a commuter. Well, needless to say, this brown-eyed, self-contained wonder dog adjusted like he has to everything else that has been thrown at him. Hunter is now a regular commuter to NYC.

Eric told me he believes Hunter's self-contained demeanor, intelligence, and his "just do it" attitude had a lot to do with his survival and ability to adapt. Hunter stays quietly on the floor while Eric is working, but somehow—at just the right time and only with the right person—Hunter will crawl up on the sofa next to a client. He always scopes out the clients first to choose which ones might find his presence acceptable. So far he has a perfect score. Hunter has never met a person he does not like, but his perception as to who would not mind his approaching them is quite amazing.

Hunter spends more time with Eric, but when Deb comes through the door, he bounds over to greet her and nuzzle her with joy. The happiest times for Hunter, though, are when all three of his family members— Deb, Eric, and Eric's daughter—are all together. This is when his life is truly complete, and he settles into his goofy sense of humor that makes them all laugh out loud.

No one knows exactly how far Hunter has come since we don't know anything about his life before the accident. What *is* measurable is the devotion, joy, and "just do it" attitude he and his family share. Not everyone would have considered adopting a dog that had undergone major back surgery, but Eric and Deb said the surgery was never a determining factor. There is no doubt the relationship this family shares is pure magic. And there is no doubt this "just do it" dog with the big eyes has some very special powers to enchant everyone he meets.

Polo— A Good Boy...Sometimes!

Polo was a ten-year-old Chihuahua whose owners surrendered him due to a lack of time to spend with him. He was scared and shaking when he was thrown into this new life. It is not an easy thing for any animal to bridge the transition to shelter life from home life, but the abrupt change was beyond traumatic for Polo. Polo was eight pounds of pure fear, and he trusted no one now. Sensing this, Mindy—one of the shelter's staff members—took Polo from his surrendering owner and went to get him a blanket and prepare his kennel. Polo was tense and fearful, so Mindy decided to sit with Polo in his kennel to see if she could calm him. Mindy sat across from Polo, whose eyes were bugging out and every ounce of his being was saying, "I don't trust you. I don't trust anyone. Don't come near me." Somehow, though, a bond developed between Polo and Mindy from those first few minutes together—a bond that to this day is deep and strong. I have experienced this instant bonding with various animals I have met, and it always mystifies me how and why this happens. It seems, at times, as an act of a more powerful being.

Over the course of the next few weeks, Polo managed to put fear in the heart of all the other staff members who tried to comfort and care for him. He would growl and charge anyone who came near him. Volunteers were afraid to take him for walks unless one of the staff leashed him and put him back in his kennel. The only exception was Mindy. I saw Mindy and Polo together on more than one occasion—Polo in Mindy's lap kissing her and looking at her like she was his salvation.

His big eyes were at ease, and his whole body was relaxed during those times he was with this one person he did not fear. It was as though Mindy were an oasis of love and compassion where Polo knew he was safe. The staff and volunteers were cheering for Polo because of Mindy's love for him, but his outcome for adoption was looking bleak. Polo had behavior issues that were beyond most adopter's ability to handle. Mindy considered adopting Polo herself, but she had already taken home two other animals that year. Mindy feared her husband, Rob, would not agree to her bringing Polo home to add to her assorted special-needs animals. One more special-needs anything seemed a bit overwhelming.

Finally, a rescue group was found who would take Polo, try to work with his issues, and find him an understanding, new home. The day came when Polo left the shelter to go to the rescue. Mindy cried to see him leave. She loved Polo with all her heart and so wanted him to have a wonderful forever home. Now she prayed that wish would be granted.

A few, short days later, however, her dream was shattered when a couple who adopted Polo from the rescue decided that he was not for them. They simply dropped him at the local pet store rather than returning him to the rescue group where they got him. Fortunately, they left Polo's paperwork with the store, and the pet store contacted the rescue group who, in turn, asked the shelter to take Polo back. This was not a very hopeful turn of events, as even the rescue did not want this poor, little boy back. There was bug-eyed, scared Polo at the shelter where he started and back with the only one in the world he loved, Mindy. Sadly, the shelter was at the end of their options, and Polo's future was very bleak.

And so it was that, with no other choices, Polo became part of Mindy's truly wonderful and unique menagerie. Mindy called him her "little drama boy," and they headed home to see if they could make this work. Mindy and Polo were now so much a part of each other that we all felt Mindy's home was where he was truly intended to live out his life.

Shortly after going home with Mindy, things got even more difficult for Polo. He had a seizure. X-rays revealed that Polo had some old fractures, but there was no specific medical evidence as to what had caused the seizure. Perhaps these old injuries had caused some neurologic damage. Suddenly, it became more evident why Polo had behavior issues. Some type of blows to the body caused these painful fractures. It seemed unbelievable that anyone could treat this little guy so cruelly.

In spite of the seizures, his mistrust of humans and his overall bad behavior, Polo began to settle into family life at Mindy's house. He loved to burrow under a blanket and take a nap in the sun on the sofa, and if Mindy was sitting close by, Polo was in a world of true joy and peace. Watching him relax made it all worthwhile for Mindy.

Life became rich for Polo again with Mindy as his light and life. Rob cannot touch Polo if Mindy is holding him without receiving growls, and Polo growls as Rob gets into bed every night. But Rob loves Polo just the same and really does not pay much attention to Polo's drama. Polo is one lucky boy to have Rob and Mindy in his life, as well as the cats, rabbits, and ferrets that share his home.

Mindy, like other special-needs rescuers, feels these special-needs animals give her the love and joy to live her life to the fullest. "These animals have truly helped me to overcome some of the difficulties that I have faced in my life," said Mindy when I asked her why she would adopt a special-needs animal.

I went to meet all of Mindy's menagerie and to visit Polo in his new family, and my heart jumped when I saw him. Mindy was outside holding him when I arrived. Polo was calm and quiet in his mom's arms. As I approached, a group of people in the street walked by the house, and he growled a very humorous growl and look up at his mom as if to say, "I am protecting you because you are all mine."

We went inside and sat down, and after some time Polo came over and let me touch and pet him. As we visited, Polo found that comfortable place in the sun and fell asleep. There was a true sense of calm and serenity in the house, even with all the dogs, cats, ferrets, and rabbits. All the animals get along amazingly well with only an occasional incident, that Mom quickly straightens out with a "come on guys" smile on her face.

Mindy shared a cute story that happened during a stormy night when she was required to stay overnight at the shelter. She brought both Polo and Sheffy, her other Chihuahua, with her to spend the night. Mindy said you have not lived until you try and sleep in a sleeping bag with two burrowing Chihuahuas. Needless to say, Mindy did not get much sleep, but the two dogs were very comfortably burrowed in the bag with their mom.

The love that glows between Mindy and Polo is quite incredible. Like all of the special-needs adopters I have been lucky enough to meet, Mindy said that she has not regretted for one minute taking Polo. And without Mindy's love and compassion, Polo would have been lost to this world instead of being safe and loved.

As I was ending my visit, Polo awoke and saw Mindy walking me to the front door. She asked me to watch what would happen next. We went out the door and looked back through the window. Polo came running and, when he saw that Mindy was already outside, he rolled over on his back and played dead. Mindy told me that every morning when she leaves for work, Polo chases her down the stairs barking and growling and then plays dead in front of the door so she cannot open it. It is as though he is hoping that if he plays dead he will convince Mindy to stay home with him. But, after a few minutes, he rolls back over and returns to the sofa to finish his nap. He is quite a character, and I saw why Mindy calls him her little drama boy.

After my visit, I knew that the world is better because Mindy and Polo are together. They have a bond that says, "I am all yours. You are my heart and my soul. And, without you, I would not be what I am." I left realizing that the world of rescue has many people and many animals who have been put together for a special reason. That made me smile as I drove away.

Mac— The Problem-Solver

I heard about Mac from a good friend, Elaine. When I told her I was writing a book about special-needs animals, she said, "Oh! You have to meet Mac." She gave me a shortened version of Mac's story, and I could not resist knowing more. Elaine introduced me to Jon and Beth, Mac's owners, at a gathering. For more than an hour they related Mac's story, and I knew I had to meet this young handsome male German shepherd who solves every problem you can put in front of him.

Beth and I planned a visit to their home. I had instructions about how Mac behaves and what to expect, and I was undaunted till I drove up the driveway. Beth had explained to me that Mac could be protective and a bit rambunctious. It was then I thought, "What have I gotten into?" Beth would keep Mac upstairs until I was inside and seated at the kitchen table. She said Mac understands that if someone is already in the house and seated that they must be OK. Once I was settled in, Beth went upstairs and let Mac out. I thought I was ready until I heard what sounded like an entire herd of deer coming down the stairs. I gasped and braced myself. When Mac burst into the room, I did not make eye contact. I waited quietly while Beth made her way downstairs and, within less than a minute, Mac was poking his head under my arm wanting attention. I started to laugh and very quickly made friends with this big fellow.

Jon, Beth's husband, had owned shepherds since his college days. Zoe, their last shepherd, had passed away several years before, but their aging Tonkinese cat made them hesitant to get a new dog right away. After a few quiet years with only the cat, he passed away. Shortly afterward Beth and Jon began to look on the Pet Protectors, Inc. website for another shepherd to fill their ranks. Beth soon found a dog named Hans at an animal control facility a little distance away from where they lived. She contacted them, and the staff member she spoke to was happy to learn they had shepherd experience. She made an appointment for Jon and Beth to meet Hans, but then said that their animal trainer would need to be there. This comment set up a bit of a red flag, but Jon and Beth were undaunted.

Jon and Beth set off to meet Hans that Saturday. They learned that he had been found abandoned and tied to a tree and was taken to the local animal control facility, but not much else was known about him. He was in good condition, bright, and alert, with true German Shepherd spirit. He did not acknowledge Jon or Beth during the first part of their visit. He was totally focused on the trainer and the tasks she gave him. Then after he went thru his paces with the trainer he came over to Jon and nonchalantly peed on his leg and sat down quietly with a bored expression. Not a very auspicious introduction, but Jon and Beth both felt that with Jon's long experience with German Shepherds they could handle whatever Hans threw at them. Little did they know what was about to happen to their lives.

After filling out the required paperwork, Jon and Beth followed the trainer's instructions to leash Hans in the back of their SUV, rather than letting him sit in the backseat with Beth. On the way home, they stopped at the local pet supply store to buy a crate, another recommendation from the shelter trainer. Beth left Hans with Jon and went in to buy the crate, thinking this would be the easiest plan. When she got back to the car, Jon looked ashen. He had let the dog out to relieve himself and noticed that Hans had eaten almost through the leash. It was a miracle the leash had not given way during the walk. Jon took Zoe's old leash he had brought and put it on Hans, hoping he would not chew through this one as well.

The animal control folks had told Jon to walk Hans for two to three hours before letting him into the house, as they did not think Hans had ever been inside a home before. So Jon walked Hans for three hours on their street and property before bringing him in. Beth said they should have walked him longer, for when they brought Hans into the house, he was frantic and began counter surfing in the kitchen like a bear raiding a picnic site. He was completely beside himself and difficult to handle. Beth said she was totally rattled by the unexpected panic attack. She admits, at this point, she thought maybe they should just put him in the car and drive back to the shelter, but she knew he had already been unsuccessfully adopted to someone who returned him to the shelter and she and Jon feared what would happen if they did the same.

As the next days progressed, Hans was always on leash inside the house and was always in his crate if they were out of the house. Jon and Beth began discussing a new name for Hans. Jon is Greek, and all his dogs had Greek names so Jon suggested "Zeus." But both Beth and Jon decided this uncivilized dog did not seem king-like. They turned to Beth's Scottish ancestry and chose "Mac" in honor of Beth's mother who was a MacIver.

Their life together was progressing, but there was a learning curve—even for breed-experienced people like Jon and Beth. Beth told me the story that Jon woke up one morning looked at her and said. "We have taken on a handful haven't we?" Jon began to laugh out loud and shake his head as he realized the enormity of the task that lay ahead of them. Mac was a big unruly guy who only knew the command "sit." That was not going to be enough if they were all going to make it together. They were clearly aware that they were Mac's only chance at life, and they took the task very seriously. They learned that Mac really did not mind the crate and particularly liked it during the day, which led them to believe Mac might have been a junkyard dog who was crated during the day and let out at night to protect a business property.

Next on their list was trying to figure out how they could allow Mac the run of their large property for his exercise. They tried an electric fence. The trainer had to increase the voltage three times before Mac paid any attention to it. If he saw a deer or animal, off he went right through the fence. Thankfully, Mac is smart and a problem-solver, and he soon learned where his territory began and ended. His job soon became clear to him; he figured he was to patrol the property and make sure no deer or squirrels or animals came into his yard. No longer was his focus going out of the yard but, rather, keeping others from coming into the yard. And Beth and Jon say he does an excellent job of it. The deer and wild animals have also learned not to come too close to Mac's territory. They joke about having the only yard in the neighborhood that has no deer, squirrels, or other wild animals visitors.

Things began to settle into a normal life. Jon and Beth developed an exacting routine for Mac, and they began to notice that he was a problem-solver. This is so true of the breed. They are smart and can do almost anything when trained.

One day Beth decided to leave Mac out of his crate and go outside for a while to see what he did. She stayed outside an hour and expected the worst when she walked back in the house but, to her sur-

prise, Mac had touched nothing. His bag of food was on the floor, and his box of treats was still on the counter when she came back in. She says it was as if Mac had turned a corner and finally understood his new life. He had his routine and his jobs to do, and Mom and Dad were always coming back home to him.

It took Mac six months to learn how to walk up stairs, so it was apparent there had been no stairs in his life. Now he may sound like a herd of deer going up and down, but the navigation of the stairs themselves is a piece of cake. From the time Mac arrived, he had adopted Zoey's old bed, and that seemed to be his safe haven when he was new to living in a house. Beth bought Mac his own fancy memory-foam bed recently, but Mac chewed it to shreds to clearly send the message that Zoey's old bed was his security place in the house and he did not want a new bed. He wanted his old bed. And so Mac's destroying the new bed was another problem solved..

I sat for several hours watching Mac and Beth interact, and I was fascinated by Mac's complete attention to anything Beth did or said. He watched her every move and obeyed her slightest command. When she went toward the refrigerator for their daily game of "Hide the Frosty Paws Treat," Mac sat at attention, his eyes not moving from Beth. Beth commanded Mac to sit, which he did. Then she went to the far end of the house to hide Mac's treat. Mac's head tilted as she walked away, but he never moved a muscle until she came back into the room and gave the command that he could go retrieve his prize. It didn't take Mac long to locate the treat, as Beth admitted she was running out of new places to hide it. Mac brought the treat back to the kitchen, and I enjoyed watching him get the Frosty Paws out of the cup. That didn't take long because Mac is an amazing problem-solver after all.

Mac is really a beautiful sight to behold. He is loving, obedient, and beyond bright. Beth joked that Mac would be totally happy if she could spend all day thinking up problems for him to solve. As I looked at his beautiful face and keen, intelligent eyes, I realized that Mac was a huge special-needs dog when he arrived. Even today he is has special needs to maintain his behavior. And I also realized that Mac was a special-needs animal that was far beyond the scope of many people who might have tried to take him on. Some had already failed. But I realized that, more than anything, Beth and Jon were very responsible pet owners. They were determined and never wavered in their commitment to Mac. As I watched this beautiful dog, I could not help finding it hard to imagine that he had ever been any other way than what he was now. When I told Beth that I could not fathom Mac being ill behaved, she just laughed at me.

I asked Beth why they did not just turn right around and take him back to the shelter. She said she knew that she and Jon were his only hope, and she and Jon could not let go of that. When I asked her if she ever regretted taking on this very special-needs boy, she said, "Not even for a minute." Beth says Mac is really Jon's dog, but it was very apparent in watching Mac with his mom the he loves Beth more than words could ever express. His beautiful eyes conveyed that message every time he looked at her. Dogs who have behavior special-needs do not always have happy endings, but the ending of Mac's tale is one of pure joy because of the love and dedication of two very special people.

Abby— The Pixie Cat Who Sneezes

I was attending a local shelter thank you lunch one beautiful spring day when I heard the shelter's animal control officer talking about some of their most memorable special-needs animals. My ears pricked up when she mentioned a cat named Abby. Because most of my rescue experience has been with dogs, I had found only one other special-needs cat story to retell. When I started listening to Abby's story, I knew I wanted to meet her and her adoptive mom.

Abby was taken to the shelter by a kind person who found her roaming the street. She was friendly, but no one knew anything about her except she appeared to be ill. She was very small, she sneezed continually, and a green discharge came out of her nose. Needless to say, her first outing after arriving at the shelter was to see the vet. The veterinarian declared that this tiny girl with the pixie nose covered in green goo had Sheep Flu and that she would probably never be free of the condition.

Abby went back to the shelter where she was loved and cared for and became a favorite of all who knew her, green goo and all. She was at the shelter for almost a year and, while everyone loved her, no one would step forward to adopt her. Abby was a lucky, little girl to be in a shelter that did not give up on sick animals. Abby was friendly, outgoing, and loveable, and no one was going to give up on her, but it was looking very unlikely she was going to be adopted. How truly sad that seemed for such a loving, little pixie girl.

Then one day her future mom, Jeannie, came to the shelter after having lost her special male cats, Zack and Max, at different times within the last year. Jeannie said she just stopped by to have a look, because she

very much missed her boys. Zack and Max were still so much a part of her heart she was not sure she was quite ready to adopt another cat, but she wanted to look. There was Abby—with her little, turned-up nose and adorable, pixie face—and Jeannie said she was completely taken with her. She learned about Abby's condition, and she felt sure she could find a cure for her. But the shelter did not let her leave with Abby that day. They wanted to make sure that Jeannie really knew what she was getting into if she really decided to adopt Abby.

Jeannie came back every Thursday, Saturday, and Sunday for a month to see Abby. And finally, a month later, the staff agreed with Jeannie that no one would care for Abby as well as Jeannie would. Abby went home with Jeannie, and so began the saga of their search for a cure.

Jeannie was still convinced she could work with her vet to cure Abby's condition. The early trips to her vet brought a new diagnosis of herpes, and Abby was put on a six-week cycle of interferon, an antiviral treatment. Jeannie hoped for a quick cure but, sadly, Abby was no better after the treatment. Undaunted, Jeannie did not give up. The vet ran some more tests, including a cat scan, ballooning her sinuses, and other tests to get to the root of the problem. Jeannie did extensive research on the Internet and continually worked with her vet to see if they could figure how to repair Abby's sinuses. They finally came to the conclusion that Abby's sinuses were damaged beyond repair, nothing could be done to make this condition go away. Whether Abby had Sheep Flu or herpes, her sinuses were impaired, and she would have to battle the recurring infections.

Jeannie loved Abby with all her heart—green goo and all—and she would have to accept Abby's condition. She would do everything she could to make her comfortable, keep her healthy, and give her the best life she possibly could. Abby and Jeannie were setting sail on a major journey to have a good life together. While Jeannie told me her story, I could see that in her failure to find a cure, Jeannie found an even greater determination and strength to see to it that Abby had as happy and normal a life as she could possibly provide her—even if that meant keeping tissue boxes all over the house and wiping Abby's nose every time she sneezed. Jeannie told me that she never once considered taking Abby back to the shelter, even though her efforts to find a cure had failed. They were a loving pair, and that was all that really mattered to either one of them.

When Abby first arrived at her new home, Jeannie opened the carrier, and Abby immediately jumped out, hopped up on the footstool in front of the fireplace, and made herself completely at home. When I visited, there was Abby in that very same place, high up and keeping watch on her mom and me. Abby weighed four and one-half pounds when Jeannie first took her home and, while Abby is still small, she is now very healthy-looking, with a beautiful, shiny coat and the brightest, elfish eyes that say, "Here I am, and aren't I the cutest thing you have ever seen?"

Jeannie apologized for all the tissue boxes around the house. She said she often has to grab for one when Abby sneezes. Abby, however, seemed completely unaware of her condition and completely at ease with her many sneezes and green goo. It is just a part of her everyday existence.

We sat chatting, and Jeannie told me all about Abby. She said she can't wait to get home from work each night to play with Abby. They play till it is time to go to bed. Abby cannot smell because of her deteriorated sinuses, but Jeannie says she still loves to eat. Abby often picks her food out of her dish with her paw and puts the food into her mouth. Jeannie thinks the extra tactile sensation compensates for Abby's inability to smell her food. Abby is unbelievably affectionate and, after I was there for a few minutes, she jumped up on the sofa and came over and sat right next to me to be petted. Abby is no standoffish cat to be sure. She is, in fact, a true "people cat." Perhaps it was all those months of surviving alone in the world that makes Abby so happy for the touch and companionship of humans.

Abby often has bouts of sinus infection, but there is no feeling sorry for her when you see how active she is and how happy she is with herself. And, while never fun, Jeannie has learned to deal with the bouts of sickness to shorten their duration. There is, of course, no cure, but as you get to know Abby, it is just one of those cute quirks about her, and you totally forget about it. Her personality far overshadows her condition. Sneezing is just part of Abby's daily routine, and she never thinks about being anything but happy. Abby's happiness rests in being with the person she loves most in the world, Jeannie.

I turned to Jeannie and said, "She looks like a little elf." As I said "elf," Jeannie said "pixie." We laughed, as both descriptions fit her perfectly. She is a pixie-elf. Her small frame and turned-up nose just make you smile. One thing that is perfectly apparent in this relationship is that there are no regrets and no feeling sorry for anything. There is just Jeannie and Abby grasping every wonderful moment they have together.

Abby and Jeannie are an incredible example of how a special-needs animal can be so loving and so giving and so special in one's life. I wondered when I left how long—if ever—it would have taken for Abby to be adopted if Jeannie had not taken her. I quickly put that thought away when I reflected on the wonderful life this duo was enjoying together.

Spike— The Crypt Keeper

One gray winter day in 2009, a woman arrived at the shelter with a scraggly, old poodle that, she said, was seventeen years old. She wanted to have him put to sleep because he slept all day and had no quality of life. She came with no medical records; he had not been to the vet in years because the family was busy travelling. Thankfully, the shelter does not euthanize dogs because of age. Allyson, our shelter manager, agreed to take this sad-looking guy, but she would not agree to euthanize him as there were no visible signs or medical records of any medical conditions. When she signed in this funny-looking dog she learned his name was Spike. She did wonder, in her heart, who would ever adopt this seventeen-year-old, scraggly looking dog.

Spike was calm and quiet on his first day at the shelter, and he seemed rather sad to find himself homeless. It is hard for a dog that has lived in a home all his life to suddenly live in a shelter with lots of noise and strange smells and people he has never seen before. But on the second day, Spike began to blossom and to show his will to be happy. His attitude grabbed the attention of everyone who came in contact with him. Spike seemed to come to life in this place where people cared about him and paid attention to him. Spike had no realization of his age, his conditions, or how funny he looked. He did not care about those things. This new world was his protective oyster shell, and he began to make the most of it. Spike immediately became a staff and volunteer favorite. Sadly, just as Spike was beginning to enjoy his life again, he had an explosive case of diarrhea, and Allyson quickly realized something was very wrong.

Following her best instincts, Allyson decided to begin some of the medical procedures needed to eventually put Spike up for adoption. As she began the process, she again wondered who would adopt Spike. His exam showed that he had a massive infection in his mouth from lack of proper care. Due to the harm done by the infection, he needed his teeth pulled. He also needed a massive dose of antibiotics to fight the infection that was raging through his body. While Spike was under anesthesia for the teeth extractions, he was neutered just in case he would make it to the adoption room. We don't often see a seventeen-year-old dog neutered, but it was a shelter rule that he would need this procedure before being eligible for adoption. It seemed like a lot of medical intervention for this poor, old guy to endure, but it seemed like the only route to health and a new home. Nevertheless, Allyson kept asking herself if she had done the right thing for Spike. She would take one look into his eyes and see that she had.

Several days after the surgery, Spike seemed to pick up the pieces of his life and began to carve out a relationship with every person he came in contact with. This now toothless dog was bopping around the shelter as if he owned the place. And if there was a volunteer around, he seemed to manage to get himself picked up and played with, loved and walked outside. He would give any passing person a certain look that could not be ignored, and he played it for all it was worth.

One day Allyson's partner, Ned, came to the shelter and met Spike. Ned too fell under the spell that Spike cast on everyone he met. Allyson decided that, with his personality and improved medical condition, she would finally put him up for adoption. She told Ned her decision that evening at dinner: The next day Spike would go to the adoption room. The next evening Allyson and Ned talked about Spike again. Even though Spike had been happy and playful in the adoption room, they realized that he really belonged home with them. Ned was adamant that no one would give Spike the life that they could. And so, at the age of seventeen, Spike became part of Allyson and Ned's family.

Allyson and Ned had a beagle named Rocky. Ned had always wanted a beagle or bulldog and, for his birthday one year, Allyson found a wonderful little beagle named Rocky that needed to be rehomed. Rocky came right in, took over their lives, and established his place as "king of the hill" until his first interaction with Spike. At that first meeting, Spike barked and made a mad dash at Rocky. Rocky backed up, and Spike immediately became the boss in his new home.

Allyson and Ned soon learned that Spike was a creature of habit, performing the same rituals at the same time every day. Change his routine, and he would freak out. At times this behavior drove them to the brink, they both readily admit. But then Spike would give them both his "look" and do something silly, and they quickly remembered why they had taken him home. When Spike wanted attention, he would come over to one of them and hit an ankle with his nose, spin, and hit the ankle again with his nose. Spike would keep this up till one of them would pay attention to him.

When it was time for Spike to eat, he would go over to Allyson or Ned and give a little grunting noise as an alert that it was his dinnertime. He was one quirky, little guy with one very big personality.

Spike had multiple medical issues, over the course of the next few years, that caused him to lose his fur and, as Allyson says, "He looked like The Terminator." One year Allyson and Ned decided to take both Rocky and Spike home to Indiana for Christmas. Spike did not make a very impressive sight to Ned's family since he was missing all the fur from half of his face and patches of fur from his body. They could not understand how Allyson and Ned could snuggle and kiss this creepy-looking dog.

The missing patches of fur and the cloudy eyes of old age earned Spike a new nickname, The Crypt Keeper. But, in spite of his looks, Spike was one happy, old boy who lived each day as it came. He played with Rocky and loved his mom and dad, and that was all that mattered to him. Crypt Keeper or not, Spike thought he was one good-looking, happy boy.

Allyson related that she is the only thirty year old she knows who sleeps in a king-size "crib." On more than one occasion, Spike had fallen out of bed at night, and it sounded like a sack of potatoes hitting the floor. Allyson said, "We decided the time had come to use those side rails used for kids' first beds as they learned to sleep in a bed instead of a crib. The only difference is that these rails were never coming off in Spike's lifetime." So she and Ned dealt with climbing in and out of the bed with these rails every night because they loved Spike and wanted to keep him safe.

Rocky was extremely afraid of the rails at first. He barked at them and would not go near them, but he, too, learned to deal with the rails that kept Spike from falling out of bed at night. After all, Spike was Rocky's best friend, and sometimes you need to do special things for a good friend.

Allyson's next stories made me laugh. One day she heard Spike barking like crazy outside in the back yard She looked out the window and saw spike

TAILS OF JOY

barking at a tree. The next day, Rocky took off out the door, barking like a maniac. Spike followed his best buddy, Rocky. Usually Spike used the ramp to go in and out, but in his frenzy to follow Rocky to see what all the excitement was about, he forgot about the ramp, went flying off the stairs, and face-planted right in a pile of mulch that, fortunately, broke his fall.

Moments like these tell you that at the age of twenty-one, Spike might be a bit of a senile, old man. He takes medicine every day for his skin condition and his arthritis, and he is now deaf and almost blind.

Sometimes Spike sleeps so soundly that it is hard to wake him up. But Spike would tell you age is not everything. He would tell you how wonderful his quality of life is, for an old guy. He lives each day to the fullest and eats kibble whole, in spite of no teeth. He goes to the groomer regularly to look the best he can. Spike still has so much life in him, and he so loves his family that has given him these wonderful, last years.

Shortly after I finished writing this chapter, I got an e-mail from Allyson saying that she and Ned had to put Spike to sleep after a ten-day illness. They stayed up all night with him the night Hurricane Sandy. They thought if anyone could make it through that long night, Spike could. And he did. The next morning, after the storm cleared, Allyson and Ned made their way out to the emergency vet clinic, but sadly the news was heartbreaking. Spike was throwing blood clots from his heart into his lungs. "We made the nauseatingly difficult decision to put Spike to sleep. It was the right thing for him but the hardest thing for us. We miss him so very much."

Ned said it best. "Everyone says Spike was twenty-one years old and had a good life with us. But he was with us only three and a half years. Someone else had him for the other seventeen years. So, to us, we felt we had lost our three-and-a-half-year-old, wonderful boy, not a twenty-one-year-old, senior boy."

Allyson told me that if something had to lead to the end of Spike's life, it was fitting that it was his heart. "It had to be huge to hold all the love he had for us and the love we had for him. We came home and took the rails off the bed. While it was nice sleeping without them, we would happily have done it for years if it meant keeping our Spike safe and with us longer. He really was such a special dog."

I was blessed to have known Spike and to have seen him spend his last, wonderful years with Ned and Allyson. Spike, you were an inspiration. You took the hand you were dealt and made the most of it. You were, to say the least, a joyful, old man and a joy to all who knew you.

I Think Benny Just Bit Me!

Our shelter had a fund-raising event, and part of the entertainment for the evening was a group of Broadway singers. The leader, Kristin, spoke of her beloved dog, Benny. It was pretty apparent that Benny had been the love of her life when he was alive. Her words made me a bit sad and teary-eyed that Benny was no longer a part of her life. She showed his framed picture as she sang a wonderful song to the tune of "My Funny Valentine." As Kristin sang, she looked at Benny's photo in front of her on the piano. I realize that while Benny had passed away a few years before, he was absolutely still a huge part of Kristen's heart and soul.

When Kristin finished the song, she told her favorite story about Benny. She and her husband, Andy, were having a typical marital quarrel. It was nothing terrible, but voices were raised and, shortly thereafter, Andy took Benny out for a ride in the car. When Andy came home, he said to Kristin, "I think Benny might have been upset by our arguing, and I think he bit me!" This little story made everyone at the event laugh because, apparently, Benny had only a few teeth left in his mouth. In spite of his harmless "bite," he wanted Andy to know that he was not happy that the two people that made up his world were arguing. The story pulled at my heart, and I approached Kristin and asked if she would be willing to tell me Benny's whole story. Sometime later we did meet for lunch, and Kristin and Andy and I were able to talk about the incredible love they had for Benny.

Andy and Kristin had lost their wonderful ten-year-old golden retriever that they had purchased from a breeder. Kristin described her as a totally beautiful dog. Months after their loss, Kristin and Andy began to think about getting a new dog, but this time they thought they would rescue a golden rather than purchasing one from a breeder. Kristin visited the local animal shelter to begin her search for a young, female golden retriever mix. As she walked down the line of kennels, she spotted Benny. Benny was a senior male lab shepherd mix who was anything but pretty—certainly not the beautiful, young female Kristin had set out to find.

Benny was old, slightly gimpy, had cataracts, and had very few teeth in his mouth. To top it off, Kristen says he had several warts on his head that almost look like antler knobs. She continued walking past the cages of dogs but, for some reason, Kristin could not consider any of the other animals. Benny had captured her heart and soul with his eyes. This was not the beautiful female she told Andy she was coming to find. She said that Benny's gaze captured her attention, and she was unable to resist this old, funny-looking dog.

Kristin left the shelter without Benny. That evening she spoke to Andy about Benny, but Andy was not in favor of taking on an older dog with so little time left. He, too, had his heart set on a young, pretty, female golden retriever. In spite of Andy's reservations, Kristin could not get Benny out of her mind. Every day she would go back to visit him, and she said, "My heart would start beating before I got there in anticipation of seeing my beloved boy." The shelter staff could see that Kristin had fallen head over heels for Benny. The only hurdle that remained was convincing Andy that this was the dog for them. One of the shelter staff suggested that Kristin take some photos of Benny and put them up around the house to convince Andy that Benny would be a good choice.

Andy took over the story from this point. He said, after four or five days, he knew there was going to be no talking Kristin out of her love for Benny, so he gave in and let her bring him home—in spite of the fact that he was not fond of Benny's old, goofy look. Even though he didn't love Benny yet, he loved Kristin, so he and Kristin went to adopt Benny.

Andy made one stipulation: They would take Benny to the vet on the way home to have him medically checked out, to get him bathed, and to have his very long nails cut. This was reasonable since Benny had been a stray picked up on Benson Road (which is how he got his name). Kristin really did not want to leave him alone at the vet, but she turned to him and said, "Benny, you have got to do this on your own so we can be together.

Your dad insists on it." Benny cocked his head and gave her a look that said, "Don't worry, I can handle it." Benny did, indeed, cope just fine with his visit. When she picked him up, Kristin received the good news that Benny had nothing seriously wrong with him, and a bath and grooming had done wonders for him.

In spite of Andy's original doubts, Benny soon became Andy's best friend and vice versa. Benny had been on his own as a stray for quite some time before he was adopted. So when Andy came in the first morning to wake Benny, the dog was startled and seemed afraid Andy was going to shoo him away. The next day Andy came into the room and slowly began to open the curtains little-by-little to wake Benny more gently.

Benny made friends with some senior citizens when he and Andy went on walks down to the shore. Andy and Benny always sat by their senior friends for a while. Andy explained that Benny did not hear or see too well and had a bit of a limp, but he was doing OK. One senior turned to Andy and said, "Us, too!"

Kristin and Andy believed that Benny had been an outdoor dog and had probably not had a lot of human attention, but it did not take him long to learn the fine art of mooching. Benny was missing some teeth, and his tongue always stuck out of the side of his mouth where they were missing. He soon learned to use this funny look to score treats. One day Kristin was escorting Benny out of the vet's clinic. When they walked past the lunchroom, Benny stuck his head in at the door and looked at one of the vet assistants who was eating a slice of pizza. Benny sat and wagged his tail, hung out his tongue, and tilted his head until the guy said, "I already gave you half my sandwich." Benny had perfected the fine art of mooching.

In the evenings, Benny greeted Andy with his tail wagging so fast it moved in a circle. He would sit between Andy's legs on the front steps and, together, they would watch the world go by. Benny loved this. It was hard for Benny to move quickly, but he would make every effort to roll over when Andy scratched him. Andy became Benny's best buddy, and Kristin was Benny's soul. "We spoiled him rotten," Kristin says. Andy took Benny to work, but no one there thought he was too neat. Andy no longer cared what they thought, because he thought Benny was the best dog ever.

Six months later, Benny had a stroke. He became more wobbly, and his bark became hoarse. But Benny was Benny, and he loved his life with his mom and dad. Benny walked with a tilted head after his stroke. It seemed to be his way of adjusting to it. He had balance issues, so Andy and Kristen adjusted each of the rooms in the house to accommodate his growing infirmities. Andy and Kristen loved Benny to the moon and back so arranging rooms for function instead of beauty did not give then a second thought.

Andy and Kristin decided they would start looking for a younger dog to adopt that might actually help Benny. They found Honey, a one-year-old golden, through a golden retriever rescue. Andy, Kristin, and Benny piled into the car and headed out to Massachusetts to meet Honey. Benny spent the time there sniffing the trees, completely ignoring his new sister. In the car ride home, he paid no attention to this beautiful, young dog. Andy laughingly described them as the "Big Log" and the "Little Twig." When they arrived home, Benny quickly accepted Honey's presence in the yard that had been Benny's alone for six months. Honey crawled into Buddy's favorite spot in the pachysandra. Buddy calmly moved to a new spot under the azalea and shared his territory with this beautiful, young dog.

Honey was very social and she wanted to approach everyone she met. Benny's life on the other hand revolved around Andy and Kristin. They were quite a pair, the Log and the Twig. When Kristin had her music students in the house for lessons, Honey was there to socialize with the kids, but Benny just looked on. Benny only wagged his tail for Andy. But life settled down into a routine, and the Log and the Twig became friends, in spite of all the differences.

Just about a year after Benny found his forever home, he became seriously ill. Andy rushed him to the all-night vet clinic, clinging to the hope that nothing would happen while Kristin was away on a business trip. Unfortunately, Benny had a ruptured ulcer, and there was nothing that could be done for him. Andy held Benny tightly as the vet administered the drugs that would end his suffering. He was with his best buddy, and there was great love and peace between the two of them even at this most difficult moment. Kristin said, somehow, she knew something was wrong. Even though she was many miles away, she was Benny's soul mate to the end.

Andy and Kristin chatted on with me about Benny as though he were still with them, even though their time together had been all too short. It was obvious that he will always be a part of them. They regaled me with more funny stories about Benny, but my favorite is still the one Kristin told that first night when Andy said," I think he bit me." I laughed at that goofy, old dog who communicated to these two people he loved, "This is my world, and please don't do anything to disrupt it."

Benny touched Andy and Kristin's hearts and souls in a way nothing else had. What greater honor could they bestow on Benny than to bring him to life with each story they tell about him. They made Benny come alive for me and I felt very honored that they shared Benny with me.

Can I Exchange This Dog for a Cat, Please?

I met Sharon through a mutual, animal-loving friend. I had told my friend that I was looking for a special-needs cat adoption story to include in my book. She told me I had to meet Sharon, and so she arranged for us all to have dinner together one evening. It was an incredible evening, listening to her stories of the many special-needs cats she had loved and cared for when no one else would. When I asked her why she had a special place in her heart for these unwanted animals, I heard an amazing story that I knew I wanted to tell.

Sharon was diagnosed with a chronic disease at the same time she moved to a new town and a new home. She was anxious, frightened, and a bit lonely as she pondered her new situation, but she found she had a deep desire to have a pet to nurture and help her get through this difficult time in her life. Her husband had always wanted a dog so, one day after work, she stopped at a local shelter and found a wonderful, little beagle puppy that she and her husband felt would be just the right animal for them.

After several weeks of puppyhood, Sharon realized she was not ready for this little ball of energy. She returned to the shelter to see if she could find a friend to nurture who was a bit less needy. As Sharon was walking through the cat area, her eyes fell on Jazzy. Jazzy was a Turkish Angora cat that completely stole her heart. After spending a bit of time together, Sharon exchanged the feisty beagle puppy for the beautiful, little cat.

During her visits to the shelter, Sharon met the shelter's district manager and the women instantly hit it off. So began Sharon's journey into the world of catdom. There would be no more pet exchanges, but there would be many more cats that would enter Sharon's life—and many of them would have special needs.

Sharon decided it would be great to adopt a cat to keep Jazzy company. She soon adopted Oreo, and things seemed just perfect for their four-member family. Life was good and Sharon found nurturing Jazzy and Oreo was helping her cope with her own problems.

Then, one day, Sharon found Emerald (Emmy) on one of her periodic visits to the shelter. Emerald was a tiny, five-pound peanut, who at nine years old and with a stage-four heart murmur, had little chance of adoption. This little girl totally pulled Sharon's heartstrings, and she knew she had to step up and take Emmy home.

Sharon's first concern was to get Emmy to eat, and so began a ritual of Emmy jumping up on a little stool in Sharon's kitchen and eating from Sharon's hand. Emmy seemed to think the food was much more interesting when lovingly fed to her piece-by-piece by her wonderful mom. Sharon never saw the lengthy feeding process as a chore. She thought it forged a strong bond of love between the two of them. Emmy's life with Sharon did not last long enough. But Sharon knew, as she said goodbye to this peanut, that she had given Emmy all the love and help she possibly could during her last months of life. "She lives forever in my heart," Sharon said.

Several more cats including Jade, Ariel, and then Kippy joined Sharon's pack as time progressed. Sharon loved all her feline friends, but Kippy stood out for her loving personality. Kippy had a stage-four heart murmur, and Sharon took her knowing she would be providing hospice care. Sharon was determined to make the time Kippy had left the best it could possibly be. Their time together was short but wonderful. Like Emmy, Kippy filled Sharon's heart with joy and love, and no task seemed to be a burden for her if it was for her Kippy. Then one day Sharon came home, and when she came through the door none of her pack came to greet here as they always did. She knew something was wrong.

When she turned the corner to the living room, Sharon saw all the cats sitting around Kippy, with Oreo sitting almost on top of her. She had passed peacefully with all her cat family surrounding her. Sharon said she could not have asked for more for her sweet, little Kippy—to be with all of her family, knowing she was loved by all who surrounded her. Though she was devastated, Sharon knew Kippy had spent her last months where she was meant to be.

Sharon's story of Shadow and Ruckus touched me deeply since they came from the shelter where I volunteered. Shadow and Ruckus were mother and son, and they were surrendered to the shelter together. Ruckus was adopted very quickly, but no one was willing to take on Shadow because she had a chronic thyroid condition.

Shadow became a regular around the place, and everyone loved her, but a shelter should never be any animal's permanent home. So, one day, our shelter manager approached Sharon to see if she would consider taking Shadow. Since Sharon was experienced in caring for special-needs cats, she did not hesitate one moment before saying she would take Shadow. And so Shadow was finally going home. All the staff and volunteers who had come to know Shadow were jumping for pure joy that this adorable girl was going home with someone they knew would love her and never think of her as just a special-needs girl.

A few months later, something very strange happened. The people who had adopted Ruckus, Shadow's son, returned him to the shelter. He had developed the same thyroid condition as his mother. Knowing that he would be a difficult adoption, the staff sent him to a feral care rescue. Shortly after, Sharon heard about Ruckus during one of her usual visits to the shelter, and she made immediate plans to go meet him.

Mother and son had been separated for two years, and when Sharon saw Ruckus she felt a huge responsibility to make sure they were rejoined. "Shadow and Ruckus just belonged together and it was up to me to make it happen," Sharon told me.

It seemed to be true fate that Shadow and Ruckus should be reunited in Sharon's loving care. To Sharon's amazement, the two acted as if they had never been separated for a moment, let alone for two years. "I could feel the joy and happiness they both felt when they first saw each other again," said Sharon.

Ruckus died after only one year with Sharon, and Shadow died three months later. Shadow just seemed to give up after Ruckus left her again. But Sharon feels quite sure that they are together, once again, in a better place. Their time together was extraordinary for them—and for Sharon who watched them reconnect vand draw strength from each other and from her. "Some extraordinary force seemed to will these two together," said Sharon.

After losing Shadow and Ruckus, Sharon felt it might be time for a break from new adoptions, but that was not to be. Even though Sharon was not seeking new adoptions, needy cats seemed to gravitate to her. Bootsy, a feral cat, found Sharon. And, then, so did Dante, a little roughneck who has scared Sharon from time-to-time by disappearing for days at a time. Just when Sharon feared the worst, Dante would show up again on Sharon's deck with a scratch on his face from some brawl he had been in.

Chi and Zul came next. They were a pair of senior Siamese cats who were overlooked by all because of their age. Plus the two had been together all their lives, and the shelter wanted to adopt them out together. Adopting two senior cats was a daunting thought for most, but not to Sharon. Just like Shadow and Ruckus, Sharon knew these two had to stay together and never be split up so she opened her home to another pair.

I spent a good portion of one day at Sharon's house as we talked about all the cats—and especially the special-needs cats—that have come through her life. Emmy, Kippy, Shadow, and Ruckus were gone, but they were still so alive in Sharon's heart. She told me that she would never have traded one moment of her time with these four cats, because they helped her so much in coping with her own issues. Sharon said, "When you worry about something whose needs are greater than your own, it makes it easier to cope with your own issues." And then I understood why her care for these special-needs cats was so great.

Sharon's house had a Zen-like quality of calm and organization. Five of the cats were sitting in the bay window soaking up the sun. Jade, who is still with her, is the alpha cat and swats anyone he feels is in his way—but it is a loving kind of swat. Chi was sleeping next to me, with her head on my leg, and Zul was asleep in the next chair.

Emmy, Kippy, Shadow, and Ruckus were all there in spirit. You could feel it and hear it in the words Sharon used in talking about them. It was all so peaceful and serene and loving. And just then we heard a loud thump at the back deck door, and there was Bootsy who wanted to come in and see what was going on. Bootsy made me laugh with his attention-seeking antics of banging on the door. Sharon opened the sliding, glass door, and Bootsy entered the room and took his place with all the others.

I spent a wonderful afternoon with Sharon and her group. I believe it is Sharon's love and compassion for these animals that allows her pack to live in harmony. She has adopted nine special-needs and older cats, and they all require medication and extra vet visits. Sharon said, "I simply add these things to my to-do list without a second thought. The unconditional love they give in return is priceless. It makes me look deep inside myself and pull out all the love and warmth and comfort that I have to share with these beautiful animals. Knowing and caring for them enriches my life. Together we have had an amazing journey and I feel blessed they all chose me."

As I pulled away from Sharon's house, the crew was still there in the bay window basking in the afternoon light together. I felt blessed that I had met Sharon and that she had shared her love of cats with me. She taught me a great deal about them, and she showed me how important they all are in completing her life. When the hard work of caregiving is not "work" but "love," it is a gift beyond compare. This kind of gift is given without strings or promises attached. It allows Sharon to place herself second and makes any task possible.

How Many Yorkies Did You Say You Have?

It was an event day at our shelter, and volunteers were needed to work the five-dollar dog wash. Maria, another shelter volunteer, and I signed up for the two-person team. I am not sure what we were thinking because, not surprisingly, we had a lot of takers for a five-dollar dog wash to raise money for the shelter. Before very long, we discovered that the people with very large dogs found this offer particularly appealing. By midafternoon Maria and I were soaking wet, and our backs were beginning to give out from lifting all those big dogs into the bathing tub. After we finished washing a particularly large shepherd mix, Maria brought in our next victim. I was totally delighted and surprised to see her return with a very cute (and very small) one-eyed Yorkshire terrier named Toby.

Maria explained that this sweet-looking, one-eyed dog came from our shelter. Her best friend, Cindy, had adopted him a few months earlier. Well this tiny boy was a far bigger challenge than any of the bigger guys we had washed. Toby was feisty and wiggly and not at all interested in looking and smelling better. But he made us both laugh, and we did the best we could. The blow dryer pushed Toby over the edge, so we spent a long time trying to get him towel-dried. To say he was our least successful client of the day would be an understatement. He looked pretty bedraggled when we returned him to his mom thirty minutes later, but she totally understood and graciously gave us her five dollars.

Toby's captured my heart with his feisty, big-boy attitude, and I decided I wanted to know more about this one-eyed wonder boy. His story—like so many rescue dogs—is sketchy at best, but I learned that Toby was five years old when his owner surrendered him when she could no longer afford to pay for all of Toby's medical issues. But the story of his missing eye remained a mystery.

The first issue the shelter had to address was a case of bladder stones. The shelter vet removed the stones, and then Toby was ready for adoption. Maria immediately called her friends Cindy and Jill, who already had two Yorkies. Maria must have been very persuasive because, several days later, Toby went home with Cindy and Jill to join their other Yorkies, Haylee and Tyler.

The very day after bringing Toby home, Cindy had to take him to the vet to remove one of the stones that had been missed in the initial surgery, since it was lodged in his penis—not an auspicious start to Toby's new life. Toby, who had been completely housebroken, began to dribble urine as a result of the second surgery. Though surprised and a little concerned by Toby's new problem, Cindy was undaunted, and she quickly learned how to diaper Toby. He is now quite an endearing sight to see with his one eye and diaper.

Jill and Cindy soon learned that Toby had another issue—fear. Cindy and Jill worked hard to help him overcome his many fears, including his fear of men. "Toby has come a long way, and has really flourished in the years since, and he actually likes men now," smiled Jill. So Cindy, Jill, Haylee, and Tyler opened their hearts and their home to this one-eyed dog with a diaper who needed a lot of love, understanding, and patience to succeed at his second chance at life.

One would think that taking on a dog like Toby would have been enough for anyone but, a year later, along came Hanna. Her story is not totally clear either as she came in from a local animal control shelter to our shelter along with Tyson, her pit bull brother. Both had been abandoned and, sadly, found their way into shelter life. Hanna had a lump that the vet thought might be cancer but, overall, she was in better shape than Tyson who was almost starving to death and could barely stand up. Something about Hanna and Tyson pulled at all of our hearts. How could anyone have done this to these two wonderful animals? It did not take long for all the staff and volunteers at the shelter to come to an unspoken understanding that we would do everything possible to give Hanna and Tyson a better life.

It was love at first sight when Jill came to volunteer one day and first laid eyes on Hanna. She needed to sit down with Cindy to discuss adopting one more Yorkie. But the minute Jill heard that Hanna might have cancer, she and Cindy agreed, "Bring her home, she belongs with us."

Hanna was on her way home to start a new life with Cindy, Jill, Hayley, Tyler, and Toby. Now they were a family of four Yorkies! I was thrilled for Hanna, but my heart cried for her best buddy, Tyson, who remained behind. He was quite sick and definitely not little and cute. To top it off, he was a pit bull, so a new home would be far more difficult to find.

Once Hanna settled into her new home, her medical problems really began to show up. Jill and Cindy knew about the tumor that needed to be removed, but they found out that Hanna also suffered from anxiety and a fear of thunder. The little dog's fears and anxieties spoke volumes about her difficult past. Cindy and Jill lavished Hanna with love and attention, and Hanna improved greatly over the next few months.

Surely, Cindy and Jill thought, this would be the end of their growing family. Taking care of any four dogs is a lot of work, but caring for four with special needs—including one in a diaper—required a lot of responsibility. Cindy and Jill were up to the task, though, and life settled into a manageable routine for the next eighteen months.

Then, when they were least expecting it, Cindy learned about a little dog named Stevie who was a six-year-old male stud dog who was going to be drowned because he had gone blind and was no longer useful for breeding by the puppy mill. Thankfully, Rescue Me Yorkie Rescue took Stevie and began the search to find him a good home. Cindy later learned that an untreated virus caused Stevie's blindness. It was heartbreaking to know that his blindness could have been prevented but, what was even more heartbreaking, was the fact that they planned to drown him, in spite of the fact that he was perfectly normal in every other way.

Cindy and Jill discussed taking Stevie for quite a while. They were well aware that adopting a blind dog would be a challenge. Cindy had a lot of experience with challenges, though, and believed that Stevie deserved a chance at a good and loving life. Jill protested initially, but she was a pretty soft sell since she agreed that Stevie was one incredible boy. And so began Cindy's quest to learn all she could about how to teach a blind dog the survival skills he would need to get along in his new life.

Cindy used a halo to teach Stevie to navigate the house. When the halo hit the wall or another object, Stevie would learn he had to go in another direction. Cindy marked certain key areas with vanilla extract to teach Stevie where his safe zones are—such as his ramp down the three stairs to the family room. The family

has a swimming pool that they keep covered, unless they are outside with the dogs. Even when they are all outside together, Stevie wears an alarm collar that will signal if he falls into the pool. Stevie can swim, but he cannot see to get out, so the alarm alerts his parents to retrieve him.

œStevie always has a small toy in his mouth when he walks around. It was a sight that brought a smile as I watched him move around the house. Originally, these toys belonged to Tyler (who got a bit irked when Stevie took them) but, after a few episodes of tug-of-war, Tyler seemed to understand that Stevie needed the toys more than he did. These toys seem to fill a tactile and security need for this otherwise undaunted, little boy. .

When I first met Stevie, I was hit hard by the fact that this wonderful, little boy nearly did not make it. I had a totally new respect for what Cindy and Jill do for these animals to make sure they have the best possible life. After six horrendous years, Stevie was finally in a place where he was loved and cared for and—most importantly—respected. That realization brought tears of joy to my eyes and a sadness to my heart for the many animals that remain in those awful places where they never see the sun, touch grass, or know the touch of a loving human. Stevie truly is one of the lucky ones thanks to Rescue Me Yorkie Rescue and to Cindy and Jill.

In case you think this is the end of this story, it is not. Several months later, Cindy got a call from Rescue Me Yorkie Rescue about Zoe, a seven-year-old, four pound little girl who had a severe, terminal heart condition. They asked if Cindy might take Zoe as a hospice case. Cindy felt she had to do this and, once again, asked Jill if she would agree to taking Zoe for these last few months of her life. Jill was not crazy about the idea of adding yet another family member, but she told Cindy it was her decision since she would have the extra work of taking care of Zoe.

Zoe's condition was serious; she was dying. I wondered how anyone could be brave enough to fall in love with an animal, knowing it was a short-term situation. I am not sure I could do that, but then I met Zoe and totally understood Cindy's decision.

Cindy felt she could handle Zoe's situation, and she wanted more than anything for Zoe to have some love and quality time in her last months of life. With great medical attention and lots of love and care, Zoe way surpassed the few months they expected her to live. She was part of this special family for well over a year.

Zoe had no idea she was sick. She sometimes had difficulty breathing, and Cindy had to rush her to the vet when she became dehydrated. But, most of the time, she actually ran and played, just like the other dogs. Her eyes were bright and full of the joyful life she had. She, too, wore a diaper like Stevie and Toby but, in spite of these special-needs, she could wrap herself right around your heart. She had on a little, red sweatshirt to keep her warm the night I visited. I took one look at her and was completely in love.

Zoe was a true fighter who had two wonderful people right there with her every step of the way. As Cindy put it, "The good news is Zoe does not know sick she is. The bad news is she is very sick. In spite of all of this, we will continue to love her to the moon and beyond. Seeing Zoe as happy as she is and seeing her interact with her siblings—often ruling the roost—gives us a great sense of joy."

I will always remember the look in Zoe's eyes that said, "There is love and joy in my life, and that is all I need." She was just one big smile, that Zoe. Surprisingly, she seemed to be the leader of the pack. This tiny peanut-of-a-girl wouldn't stand for any nonsense from her brothers and sisters. I watched while she held court, sitting on the sofa while the others surrounded her and seemed to look to her for directions. "What can we do to make more noise and play harder?" Soon Zoe would be off on her next rambunctious adventure with the rest following behind her.

Even a wonderful life cannot last forever, and Zoe passed away—not from her heart condition—but from an infection. I cried when I heard the news. Then I thought about that little girl and a smile came to my face, knowing she had savored every moment of her new life with this new family. She did not know how sick she was, and she just kept moving forward bringing happiness and joy to all who knew her. She resides in a special place in each of our hearts, and I will never forget that little peanut-of-a-girl.

Not long after Zoe's passing, Rescue Me Yorkie Rescue called again and told Cindy about Lexi. Lexi was almost blind, and her current owners surrendered her because they could no longer provide the care she needed. The staff member wondered if Cindy might take her, for who could better care for Lexi than this incredible group? That is how tiny Lexi came to live with this crazy family.

Cindy took Lexi to the vet several times, and they determined that Lexi's eye condition was causing her a lot of pain. They hoped that surgery would alleviate much of the pain and, hopefully, improve her eyesight. It was a tough decision to put this little girl through a serious surgery, but—once more—Cindy and Jill put their fears aside in the hope of doing the right thing for Lexi.

Cindy experienced her darkest moment shortly after Lexi's surgery. It seemed that Lexi's eyesight had not improved and that she was now not able to see at all. Both Cindy and Jill were devastated that, in spite of their best

intentions, it seemed they had made the wrong decision. Several weeks passed, and there was little improvement in Lexi's condition.

Finally, Cindy learned from another vet that it often takes a long time for the swelling from the surgery to subside and for sight to return. She grasped this new hope and, sure enough, with another visit to the vet and some new medicine, Lexi began to see more and more each day. It had been a long, depressing journey at times, but little sunshine Lexi has come through it successfully. She has regained much of her vision and is now part of the crazy pack chasing and running and loving life to the fullest. Lexi made me smile from the moment I met her, but her recovery brought incredible joy to everyone who knew her—especially to Cindy and Jill who finally knew they had made the right decision.

I got a real sense of what taking care of these special-needs animals means to Jill and Cindy when I spent time with them. Their saga started when they purchased Hayley and Tyler from pet store. Their experience with those two grew into a love of special-needs animals. When you observe these wonderful dogs with Cindy and Jill, you would think each and every one of them was perfectly normal. They all live with a joy and dignity that is incredible to see.

Cindy is so organized that she makes it all look easy, but I know it is not. She has a room with trimmed diapers in one drawer and diaper wraps in another. Each dog has its special food and meds clearly labeled and marked. Cindy seems nonchalant about everything, and told me she felt that taking care of special-needs Yorkies was her calling. She knows that most special-needs animals are not going to be adopted, and she needs to help where others won't. Jill has worked with special-needs people and has learned to transfer this knowledge to these special-needs dogs. These two wonderful people have made a huge difference in the lives this little pack of Yorkies.

I was amazed when Jill protested that she is not a big dog-fan, due to a childhood incident. She confessed that she always has to have a get-away plan when she is with a dog. I watched her hold Toby like a baby, and I quickly realized that Jill deals with her fear because the needs of these animals are far greater than her fear. As we were winding down our evening, Jill spent a good deal of time telling me about Toby's last year. He began having seizures, which was very scary for all of them. After a lot of research, they discovered he had a calcium deficiency, which they are correcting. Even though the seizures have almost disappeared, Toby has stenosis in his legs and has become grumpy. But as Jill related all these challenges too me, she was holding Toby and kissing him. He was one very happy, little dog, wrapped in her arms.

I have known about each of Cindy's dogs as they came along, but it was only when I was began to write their story that I saw them as a unified family. I realized just how special these two people are. Cindy said that watching an animal's health improve with love and good medical care provides an incredible feeling of joy and pushes her onward.

What especially struck me, as I sat having dinner with all of them, is how very normal everything seemed. Three dogs were wearing diapers—including the little peanut with her red sweatshirt—and there was a blind dog with a toy in his mouth. Although the description sounds bizarre, the room resonated with love and joy. Both Cindy and Jill said they would not have done anything differently and that the love and joy they feel helping these wonderful animals overcome their challenges is what makes everything work.

As I left that evening, I realized how lucky I was to know Cindy and Jill and how lucky all these special needs guys were to be part of this loving family. Cindy and Jill have truly made a difference in the lives of these animals, and the world is a better place because of this loving family. In return, Cindy and Jill have experienced the true joy and love that comes with caring for a special-needs animal. Or, in their case, *many* special-needs animals. Thank you, both, for all you do to make this world a better place.

Chloe—
Heart of My Heart, Soul of My Soul

In the years that I have been working with and rescuing animals, especially dogs, they have taught me more than I could ever have imagined. I have spoken about many special needs animals in this book but, until recently, I had no need to talk about my own relationship with a very special girl named Chloe. To say that she and I breathe at the same time is really not an exaggeration. Chloe came into my life as a pup, several months before my husband died quite suddenly from a heart attack. Somewhere in the fog of grief, I thought about giving Chloe to my best friend Linda. Linda called her "my little loaf of bread" because she was so small and light, and she just fit under her arm when they crossed a street. Linda came to help me take care of Chloe and her sister, Lily, during the days following my husband's death. Linda is a friend like no other, and I would never have made it through these dark times without her. I was quite sure Chloe would be better off with Linda than me.

I was not sure I could manage anything in my life at that moment—let alone giving proper care to two dogs—one just a puppy. But one day as I sat crying, a miserable heap on the kitchen floor, Chloe came over to me, sat in my lap, and comforted me. How could she possibly know and understand? But she did. It was then that I knew I could never give her up. She and I were together forever. For the first few years after my husband's death, both "the girls" (as my friends referred to them) were my reason for being, and they kept me from seeing life as a dark hole.

An incredible bond grew from those days with both Lily and Chloe, but little Chloe crawled into my heart and occupied it like no other animal I have ever had. She knew my every word, and hung on my every step. She could judge my mood in a second and was there for me whatever I needed—as long as it was love. This has been our life together now for many years, and will be for all the time we have together.

Recently, Chloe experienced some illness as she entered her senior years. My happy, wonderful girl now said to me with her eyes, "Mom, I just don't feel good." Our relationship is like that. She can read me without a word, and I can read her right back. It is a very special relationship that I share with no human. So when Chloe started to experience pain and discomfort, I was devastated. She, on the other hand, seemed to accept her tiredness and lack of energy far better than I. She was fourteen years old, and I tried to accept that I was the luckiest person in the world to have had the relationship with her for as long as I did. I tried to come to grips with the fact that our time together might be winding down.

But, try as I did, I just could not accept it as well as Chloe. I took her to the vet time-and-time-again, seeking a solution. Every time I put Chloe in the car, she would sit next to me and look up at me with her wonderful dark eyes as if to say, "Don't worry so much, Mom, I am not afraid of what lies ahead." She seemed afraid, but accepting, and I just felt afraid and beside myself. I wanted to include this chapter about Chloe in my book, as now I truly knew what it was to care so much for a special-needs animal.

For four months we struggled through tests and experiments with various medicines, but nothing made her much better. We were now at a crossroads of whether to choose invasive testing, since none of the noninvasive testing resulted in any clues as to what was wrong.

I had thought long and hard about this choice and, with the help and advice of my vet, we decided that invasive testing was not the right thing to do for Chloe. She was fifteen years old and, even if we found something, I did not want to put her through a difficult medical treatment. I was chasing an answer because it was the right thing for me. I was not ready to say good-bye. But I knew in my heart that I had to do what was right for Chloe. I did not know how to accept the fact that we had no answer. I just could not give up.

Then, one day, Chloe looked at me with her sweet, loving eyes, and she and I both agreed that what would be would be. She taught me to accept our situation, and it brought me more peace and love than I had ever known. Our time together had been better than either of us could ever have imagined. Now I realize each day is precious. She is the heart of my heart and the soul of my soul. Now, even with her special needs, I would not change one moment of the time we have had together.

As a last idea, my vet suggested we try switching Chloe to a novelty diet of things she had never eaten before. She thought that perhaps she had developed an allergy to some of her food. I grasped at that straw, as I had nothing else to hold on to. After weeks of no appetite, Chloe began to eat her new diet—duck, venison, and rabbit. Within a week, I began to see my old, wonderful girl begin to slowly come back. She would run to the door for her walk and prance down the street as she used to. She ate with gusto, rushing to the kitchen the moment she heard the refrigerator door open. My little eleven-pound dog was eating again.

As Chloe improved, my heart and my soul were lifted to such a joy it cannot be put into words. But I was afraid to hope for too much. I have her back now, at least for a little while longer, almost the way she was. Now she has lost some of her hearing, and she cannot hear the refrigerator door opening or hear me call her from another part of the house. She does not have the strength and coordination that she used to have when she would fly from one spot to the next. She is wobbly when she first gets up from her now very long naps, and she occasionally misses her jump up onto the sofa. She sleeps more than ever, but once she opens those beautiful, dark eyes, my heart leaps for joy. No one would ever know that she is hard of hearing the way she compensates with her other senses. In spite of all the changes, Chloe still enjoys her walks in the sun, her time sitting next to me just sharing the same space, and her joy in stealing a bite of whatever I am eating.

I have learned a very important lesson from all of this. My time with Chloe is limited I know, but I have learned to make each moment and day count and to cherish and love the things the two of us can still do together. I love the feel of her when she gets on the bed and curls up next to me. I no longer take it for granted, but instead, I say a small thank you for this extra time we have together. She has taught me what is important in life, and it is very different than what I had thought was important. I know the time will come when we can't make her well, but I believe she has taught me the grace to accept it as she will do when that time comes.

Chloe, you are the greatest gift I was ever given, and I want so much for you to be proud of your Mom. You have taught me well.

Heart of my heart, soul of my soul, I love you, dear one, more than you will ever know.

Made in the USA
Lexington, KY
26 October 2014